MĀṆḌŪKYAKĀRIKĀ

This book was originally published in Italian
as, Gauḍapāda, *Māṇḍūkyakārikā*, by Edizioni Āśram Vidyā, Rome

First published in English in 2002
by The Aurea Vidyā Foundation, Inc.
325 Canal Street, New York, N.Y. 10013, U.S.A.
www.vidya-ashramvidyaorder.org

Set in font ©Vidyā 11/13 points by Aurea Vidyā

Printed and bound in the U.S.A.
by Sheridan Books, Ann Arbor, Michigan

ISBN 1-931406-04-9
Library of Congress Control Number: 2002113021

On the cover: *Śiva Naṭarāja* (Lord of the dance), detail.

Śiva Naṭarāja (Śiva in the guise of Lord of the dance) emerges out of Black, symbolically out of the non-manifest, and represents the Nature of Being in the non-differentiated state out of which, "through dance", comes simultaneously into manifesation the world of names and forms.
Black is the non-color, luminous essence of white light. It is the symbolic fabric out of which the entire range of colors (divine principles) emerges and into which is reabsorbed.
Black also has a "decorative" valence. Decor in a traditional sense is linked to the rite of passing, the act inherent in the deposition of gross matter (death). Black, compact, clean, free of tones symbolizes Unity of all non-manifest spiritual principles, the non-place out of which the First Principle emerges.

GAUḌAPĀDA

MĀṆḌŪKYAKĀRIKĀ

The Metaphysical Path of Vedānta

Translation from the Sanskrit, and commentary, by

RAPHAEL

(Āśram Vidyā Order)

AUREA VIDYĀ

I bow to that yoga, taught by the very Scriptures, well known as Asparśa, free from relations, beneficial, generator of bliss for all beings, free of oppositions and contradictions.

Gauḍapāda

TABLE OF CONTENTS

Introduction 11

Āgama Prakaraṇa 17

Vaitathya Prakaraṇa 55

Advaita Prakaraṇa 77

Alātaśānti Prakaraṇa 97

Sanskrit text 139

Glossary 163

About Raphael 185

INTRODUCTION

The *Māṇḍūkya Upaniṣad* is part of the *Atharva Veda* and belongs to a relatively remote period. Though short, it sums up the entire metaphysical vision of the doctrine of the *Upaniṣads*.

For the "intuitive" ones this *Upaniṣad* outlines the entire *sādhanā* toward realization. It considers the metaphysical or non-qualified Being, the Being-cause or ontological One, the manifold states of the One-Being, the possibility for beings to transmigrate from one state of existence to another, the *jīva*-soul's identity with the One-Being and therefore with the metaphysical Being, and the technique of ascesis through the *mantra* AUM.

The states of the One-Being are synthesized into three states, however, the three are but a single state with a three-fold vibrational mode. This manifest unity in turn represents *one* of the infinite determinations of the metaphysical Being, of Non-Being, of the metaphysical or Absolute One, in other words, of *Brahman Nirguṇa* (non-qualified) or *Turīya* (the Fourth).

The different states of existence are "modes of being", vibratory states that express qualities; so the beings, according to the qualities they express, may find themselves in one or another vibratory state of life. To express these vibratory states in conceptual terms, the *Upaniṣad* uses specific names;

thus we have the states of *prājña, taijasa, viśva* and, for the non-conditioned or infinite state, *Turīya.*

The *viśva* plane is the dense physical state, the gross state that we are presently experiencing; the *taijasa* plane is the subtle or hyper-physical state, beyond the electronic mass. It is nto this state that we retire when we sleep and whence we will abandon our outer "garment" or gross physical body. *Viśva* and *taijasa* differ only in that they express different vibrations, just like the color violet may differ from golden yellow; they are formal states, characterized by the subject-object dualism, by cause-effect and by the condition of the individualized being. One who dwells in *taijasa,* as we have already said, has removed only his corporeal sheath, and retains all of his intellectual-volitional, sensorial and conscious faculties.

Prājña is the causal, germinal state, the noumenon of the entire manifestation; it is the seed-essence of Being. All things originate in and return to It; in *prājña* the effect, like all manifest polarities, reintegrates into the cause.

A being, in *prājña,* is its own unity-synthesis, is pure awareness without any superimposition; *prājña* is therefore a state of fulfilment, of non-desire, of total lack of duality, of non-movement. It is pure Knowledge, knowledge that no longer concerns phenomena-objects, but the ultimate Subject; a being knows itself for itself and in itself. At this level knowledge becomes awareness, not "awareness of something; it is awareness which reveals itself, since in *prājña* there are no objects or data of any order or degree.

If in *viśva* and *taijasa* reality is expressed in terms of "I am this", in *prājña* it is expressed as "I am"; the "this" (the knowable *object*) disappears, so that only the pure awareness of Being remains. When, instead, reality resolves in: "I am That", then Being, as a determination of the Absolute, is reintegrated into its non-qualified, non-determined substratum (*Turīya*).

Reintegration occurs when one awakens to the awareness of *ātman*-Self. This implies that Liberation is not a "conquest", nor is it the effect of some cause that did not exist before, because the state of unity (*Brahman-ātman*) has always existed, but for the being fallen into *avidyā*, that state is only virtual and potential.

It is necessary, therefore, to awaken to what one really and deeply is, beyond all veiling "superimposition". In the end, and from a certain perspective, even Liberation is simply a mental category from which one must be freed. *Kārikā* 32 of chapter II says:

«There is neither birth nor dissolution, nor aspirant to Liberation, nor liberated, nor anyone in a state of slavery».

The *Upaniṣad*, of great initiatory interest, acquires greater value through the addition of Gauḍapāda's *kārikās*, some of which are an integral part of the *Upaniṣad*.

Gauḍapāda divides this work into four parts, naming them:

1. *Āgama Prakaraṇa*, based on the scriptures or *Śruti*.

2. *Vaitathya Prakaraṇa*, based on the phenomenal or apparent character of experience.

3. *Advaita Prakaraṇa*, based on non-duality.

4. *Alātaśānti Prakaraṇa*, based on the extinction of the "burning ember".

In it He unveils for the first time, clearly and concisely, the *Asparśa yoga* or *vāda* (path, way), the metaphysical *yoga*, the pathway which leads not to union with the God-person, but to integral Liberation (*Turīya*).

This *yoga*, it must be clarified, requires great psychological maturity, an intelligent and keen intellectual discernment and a mind not conditioned by erudite preconceptions.

Asparśavāda is for the seekers of the ultimate Truth, for the lovers of pure knowledge or wisdom (*philosophia*), for those who seek Being and not becoming-phenomena, it is not for devotional mystics, nor for those who base their *sādhanā* on psychological and physical practices. This *yoga* is also known as *Ajātivāda* (non-generation).

Śaṅkara with his *Advaita Vedānta* continues Gauḍapāda's *Advaita* themes, expanding them with a dialectical rigor which has never been either equaled nor surpassed.

Although often degraded to the level of a simple extra-sensorial or hyper-physical condition, the term "metaphysical" in this context, as in every initiatory context, must be taken to mean beyond the gross, subtle and causal states beyond Being itself and all its manifold states.

Therefore only the Fourth state is metaphysical because Being, with its many systems of co-ordinates, is already present in the plane of "substance", of nature (*prakṛti*). The supranatural is not simply beyond the physical, but beyond the subtle and even the causal-germinal states; these belong to the natural, the formal and the non-formal plane. We must therefore be vigilant when we follow a metaphysical pathway not to mix up the para-psychological, the magical and the "astral" spheres with the strictly metaphysical one.

Raphael's commentary is only intended as an explanation for the western researcher, who may be unfamiliar with the vast philosophical themes of Hinduism and Buddhism, and is more accessible than Śaṅkara's extensive, deep and incisive commentary expounded in the *Māṇḍūkya Upaniṣad with Gauḍapāda's kārikā and Śaṅkara's commentary*[1]. From it, noumerous *Śaṅkara*'s passages are quoted in inverted commas along with the text.

---

[1] Italian Edition with notes by Raphael. Edizioni Āśram Vidyā, Rome. Italy.

«I bow deeply before this *Brahman,* who, although free of birth, appears to be born through its inscrutable power; although always at rest, appears to move; although one, appears as multiplicity to those whose vision has been deformed by the perception of the various attributes of objects, this *Brahman* destroyer of all fear for those who find refuge in It.

I greet, prostrating myself, my Master's Master, the most venerable of venerables, who, on seeing the creatures drown in the ocean of this world - an ocean infested by terrifying sharks such as birth and death - has given, out of compassion towards beings, this nectar, difficult to drink even for the Gods and which lies in the depths of the ocean which is the *Vedas,* the same *Vedas* which he reveals through the power of his illuminated intellect.

With all my heart I pay homage to my Master who destroys the fear of transmigration. Through the light of his illuminated intellect he has dissipated the obscurity of the illusions in which my mind found itself, and has broken for ever my fear of appearing and disappearing in the terrible sea of *saṁsāra.* Those who find refuge at his feet may realize the infallible knowledge of the *Upaniṣad,* peace and humility».

OM OM OM

Chapter I

Āgama Prakaraṇa

(Chapter based on the Sacred Scriptures)

OM

Salute to *Brahman*

I *Sūtra of the Upaniṣad*

Hari OM! OM is all this. A clear explanation (follows): that which is past, present and future is truly OM. And that which is beyond this threefold temporality, in truth, is always OM.

The threefold sense of time made up by past (*bhūtam*), present (*bhavad*) and future (*bhaviṣyad*) represents the totality of the manifestation of *Īśvara*, the "all this" of the *Sūtra*, and corresponds to the sound OM. But, beyond this threefold time, there is the atemporal or the non-manifest principle (*avyakta*), which is always OM.

OM is the "Word" of power which manifests and sustains the threefold world; all things originate and dissolve in It.

The non-manifest corresponds to the germinal, causal (*kāraṇa*), potential state. The entire manifestation, in all its unlimited qualitative and quantitative possibilities, is potentially contained in the primordial seed: similarly the entire tree, with its branches, fruit and leaves, etc., is contained in potency in its seed. Manifestation is the *unfolding* of the potency of the principle. The manifest objectifies or makes its potentialities emerge. One may say that the manifest "evolves" only, though, if this term is considered to mean unfolding, evolving of the seed, going from potentiality to act.

The totality of existence is contained in the "Word" or the fundamental, determined and qualified Note of Being. Seen from the point of view of Being, manifestation is a present whole; Alpha and the Omega are in Being.

II *Sūtra of the Upaniṣad*

All this is verily Brahman. This ātman is Brahman and the ātman has four quarters (pādas).

OM is *Brahman*; the "Word" is *Brahman*. *Brahman* is the original name, OM is the sound-essence. If all manifest things are OM at different vibratory levels, and OM is *Brahman*, then all beings (*ātmā*) are OM-*Brahman*. That (*Brahman*) is "I". In this *Sūtra* three things are evidenced:

- *Brahman* is the whole (but not all is *Brahman*);
- The inner Self of beings is in the nature of *Brahman*;
- *Brahman-ātman* has four parts or *pādas*.

Brahman is one and undivided, but it expresses itself in four vibratory states, in the same way as an individual, although one, experiences while in the waking state, while dreaming and in deep sleep. These, therefore, are states of consciousness, they are existential modes. Thus, if things are observed from a certain perspective, there is neither a "here" nor a "beyond", there is a Being with manifold consciousness and vibrational possibilities, that are expressed in the great total oneness of *Īśvara*. The very being's bodily "death" (transition from *viśva* to *taijasa*) is but a simple change of rhythm, of state, of co-ordinates in the apparent flow of a *manvantara*.

III *Sūtra of the Upaniṣad*

The first quarter (pāda) is vaiśvānara, whose sphere (of action) is the waking state; it is conscious of external objects, it has seven limbs and nineteen mouths; it experiences gross (material) objects.

The first quarter or *pāda* (foot) is called *vaiśvānara* (or *viśva*) and the *ātmā* experiences the gross objects on this vibratory plane or sphere. With what does it experience them? With the different senses or sensorial organs, with the "mouths", the openings or windows through which it enters into contact with the objective or gross world.

The physical body as a whole is the sheath of *ātmā* that creates the link with the gross sphere (*viśva*) which corresponds to the waking state or what goes by that name. Identification with this state and vehicle causes us to say "I am this body", "my reality is this external world of objects".

The "materialistic" vision of life originates from the identification of the consciousness-*ātmā* with this body and this vibratory state. The materialist is, therefore, an innocent child who has identified exclusively with his gross body and with the gross sphere (*Virāṭ*) of *Brahmā*. Thus his reality is of a material, empirical, objective order external to himself as the subject; hence his conditioning and alienation.

IV *Sūtra of the Upaniṣad*

The second quarter (pāda) is taijasa (the luminous) whose sphere of action is the dream state; consciousness here is interiorized. It has seven limbs and nineteen mouths and experiences the subtle objects.

The second quarter or *pāda*, is called *taijasa* and its sphere of activity is subtle or hyperphysical. *Taijasa* means luminous because this subtle vibratory sphere is shining, radiant.

The analogy is with dream; as in dream the nocturnal universe, effect of the *vāsanās*, is projected by the imagination of the *manas* (mind), so in *taijasa* the imaginative power of *manas* molds geometrical constellations of thoughts and feelings. This subtle world (with reference to the gross one of *viśva*) is characterized by the psyche aspect of *ātmā*.

Taijasa may be divided into two vibratory dimensions or spheres: the first characterized by *ahaṁkāra*, that is, by human individuality (or parallel to the human) or subhuman; and the second, characterized by *buddhi* or universal consciousness which operates through the *vijñānamaya* sheath (pure intellect). The former is dominated by the empirical mind-desire (*kāma-manas*), the second is under the dominion of superconscious intuition, of pure intellect.

In alchemical terms one might say that the former represents Mercury (☿) dominated by earth-salt (⊖), while the latter represents rectified Mercury (☿) dominated by Sulfur (🜍); or, that the former is the lunar dimension, the latter the solar one.

The *Maitry Upaniṣad* (VI, 30) says: «Quality [*guṇa*], due to the power of differentiation [innate in] Nature, becomes the soul's bondage, due to the mental determination [which is inherent in it]. Emancipation follows the destruction of mental determination, [since], in truth, it is through the mind that one sees, through the mind that one hears, [etc.]. Desire, decision, doubt, faith, mistrust, firmness, stability, shame, reflection, fear, all of these are nothing but [modifications] of the mind. Transported by the swell of the *guṇas*, unstable, mobile, distracted, avid and agitated, [the Spirit] reaches the presumption [of being a specific individual]. Formulating thoughts such as "I", or "he", or "this is mine", etc., he ties himself like a bird in a net»[1].

With *buddhi* we are in the subtle world of the... Gods; *ahaṁkāra* is not active and consciousness is able to respond to the universal rhythm of Being. On the plane of *buddhi* the *ātmā* is already "Person" more than individuality.

Manas is typical of human individuality and it is through it that *ahaṁkāra*, the sense of ego, of individuality as such, expresses itself. (See the chart on page 25). The *Kaṭha Upaniṣad* (II, III, 7-8) says: «*manas* is superior to the senses, *buddhi* is superior to *manas*, the great *ātmā* is superior to *buddhi* and the Unmanifest [*avyakta*] is superior to the great *ātmā*. But the all-pervading and informal *Puruṣa* is, in truth, superior to the Unmanifest. The being who has known it is freed and goes to immortality».

And again: «Recognize the *Ātman* as the owner of the chariot, the body as the chariot, the *buddhi* as the charioteer, the *manas* as the reins... The person who has discernment for charioteer and *manas* for reins reaches the goal, which is the sublime See of *Viṣṇu*». (Ibid: I, III, 3-9).

Taijasa, therefore, has two aspects: one represented by pure intellect (*buddhi* or *noesis*), looking up to the world of

---

[1] For this and other quotations: *Upaniṣad antiche e medie*. Boringhieri. Torino. Italy. (Italian Edition).

"Ideas", the other, represented by the imaginative mind (*manas*) looking towards the world of sensorial "representations" or shadows.

A *ray* of pure intellect (*Noûs*) takes on individuality and manifests itself as *ahaṁkāra* and *manas*.

Ahaṁkāra is a prism which refracts the universal Light of *buddhi* to produce a particular ray. *Ahaṁkāra* particularizes, differentiates what is synthesis and unity.

One might also speak of higher and lower *taijasa* to indicate the two domains, one universal, the other individual. The latter is the so-called "astral" world, in its various branches, of western occultism (astral because it is luminous, in fact). Later on, whenever reference is made to this subtle sphere, it will concern mainly the lower domain of *taijasa*.

When it abandons the gross or bodily sheath, the *ātmā* or the *jīva* retires naturally into *taijasa*; but this sphere may also be experienced even while we are in a physical body; we do experience, in fact, it but there is no memory. Many individuals, far more than one might expect, experience it consciously because, for various reasons, they are able to depolarize themselves from the electromagnetism of their dense body. Even a number of drugs may cause this passage of state, although in a passive condition. But drugs are extremely dangerous causing, as they may, the breaking of the "thread" (*sūtrātmā*) which connects the two states; this implies one's "death" to the gross-physical condition.

Official science could, if it so desired, direct its efforts and means towards the revelation of this state, this dimension, this system of co-ordinates, to the great advantage of knowledge. But science appears to be bogged down in the gross sphere exclusively, without any intention of going beyond it.

The world of *taijasa,* but also the physical world, has different vibratory states, and therefore different possibilities of life. There in accordance with their *status* of consciousness or with their attunement with the individuated or the universal, beings find their corresponding place or activity.

With regard to those who might have experienced this sphere and then have attempted a description, it must be pointed out that these descriptions should not be considered as absolute because each one of them can only describe the "environment" by which one was attracted. But this criterion is applicable also to the *viśva* plane.

Another error that is often made is that of considering a being wiser and fulfilled only because they have had experience of the other side of the veil. *Taijasa,* in its lower plane, is the intermediate sphere, that of the psychic; it is the dimension where the *kāma-manas* (emotion-imagination) rules; it is, therefore, the sphere of the fluctuating, the fleeting, the non-constant, the non-real.

Upon this subtle plane, as one may deduce, one's direction is driven by one's most pressing desires, one's unresolved qualified expressions that press forward to guide one in one's choices and direction. This is because in *taijasa* the "substance" is particularly sensitive and reacts immediately to the powers of emotion and imagination. There, one might say, emotion-imagination is all; in *viśva* the "substance" is heavier, more inert, slower, thereby not allowing its "conformation" to take place rapidly, although this is not in absolute terms.

In *taijasa* each entity creates – as in a dream, and speaking in religious terms – it's own hell, purgatory or paradise depending on the state of consciousness reached or on one's determining psychic magnetism. Thus, one may have terrifying experiences, but also exalting ones with all the in between nuances. This is in response to a universal and natural law of justice. Each one rewards or punishes oneself by oneself. One may also deduce that *taijasa* is the sphere of polar mysticism that is characterized by dualism such as creator-creature, heaven-hell, good-evil, etc. It is experimentation of certain kinds of *samādhi*, that no matter how intensely gratifying they may be, belong nonetheless to the lower psychic domain. In any case, many are attracted by it, and if one considers that each being in time-space expresses his own particular state of awareness and vibration, one may see that all things are in their proper place.

> «... when man abandons life he becomes what he wilfully conceived for himself in this world. For this reason you should train your will».
>
> (*Chāndogya Up.*: III, XIV, 1)

Lastly, knowledge does not occur through logical and conceptual analysis, as it does in *viśva* (although thought and discernment are present) but rather, thanks to a sort of "vibrational sensitivity" for the object. It is psychic receptivity of one being towards another; and, depending on the greater or lesser ability to respond, a being perceives the environment and the other beings surrounding him. It is the lower octave of the super-conscious intuition of the *buddhi*; in the upper state of *taijasa*, in fact, knowledge is the effect of intuitive discernment, of *Noûs*, it is knowledge of the archetypes-noumena rather than of phenomena.

In *prājña*, as we shall see later, knowledge is perfect identity because subject and object coincide.

Here is a summary table of *taijasa* and *viśva* with the sheaths of *ātmā*:

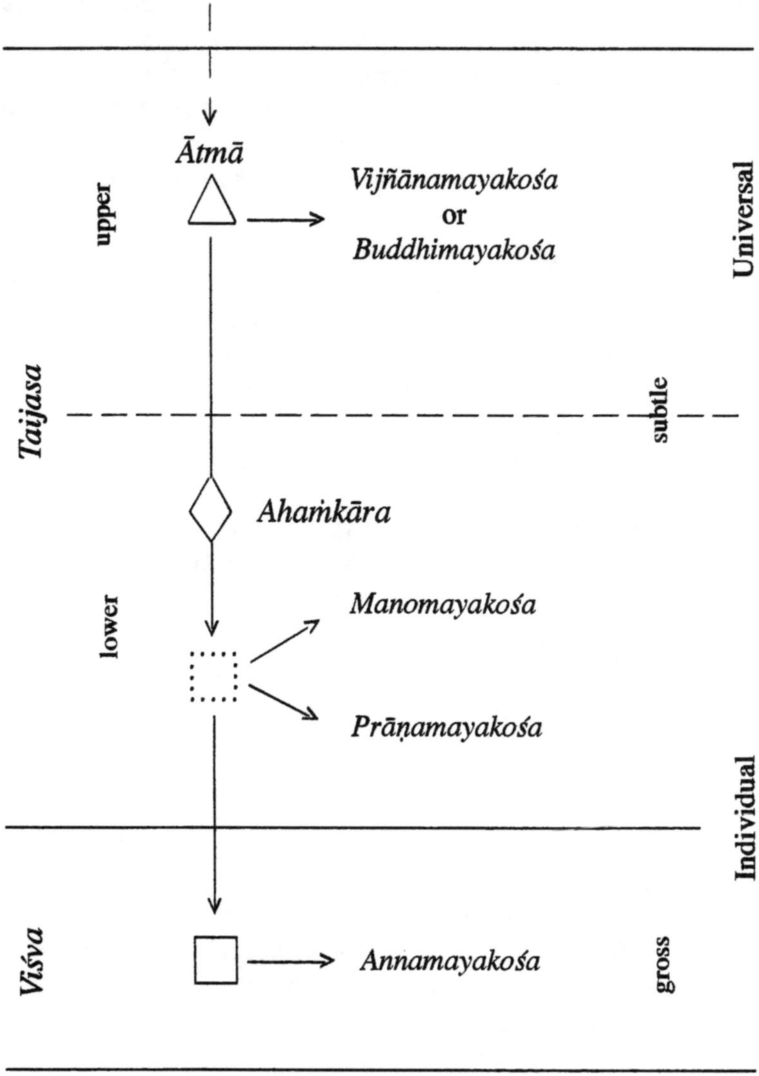

V *Sūtra of the Upaniṣad*

This is the state of deep sleep in which the sleeper no longer enjoys any object nor experiences any dream. The third quarter (pāda) is prājña whose sphere of activity is, in fact, deep sleep; here all things remain undifferentiated; in truth, it is a unity of pure consciousness. (In prājña) there is fullness of happiness and (the sleeper) truly tastes this happiness. It is the cognitive condition (of the other two states).

The third quarter or *pāda* is called *prājña*, synthetic knowledge, and is compared to deep sleep without dreams (or *suṣupti*). This is quite indicative because while in the two previous states all is characterized by subject-object, the seer and the seen, the dreamer and the dreamed, etc., therefore, by dualism, in *prājña* dualism vanishes and all is resolved into unity. Here *ātmā* is in itself, with itself and for itself, it is in the eternal present.

While in *viśva* and *taijasa* the object causes happiness, in *prājña* there is bliss without objects, therefore *prājña* is *pax profunda*, pure happiness which does not depend on external factors. The being, therefore, finds his true home there, his homeland, his proper place, his completeness without depending on anything but himself. This state is the highest *samādhi* on the plane of manifestation.

As the origin and potential germ of qualified developments, it constitutes a being's true nature-essence-noumenon, just like the seed of a flower is the flower's exact and real noumenal representation. And just as the flower is contained in the seed, so *viśva* and *taijasa* as well are contained in *prājña*. However, it is important to specify that manifestation is a simultaneous "ideation" (the example of the seed might be misleading).

It is the empirical being who, by experiencing a particular system of co-ordinates, conceives Totality as having a birth and an evolution in time. Manifestation will not grow perfect with time, it is simply the irradiation of the primordial Idea.

The Idea contains in itself the totality of life or the manifold states of existence. A planet is but a materialized Idea, an Idea with its own vibratory condition. *Viśva* is an Idea that vibrates at a particular intensity and frequency, it is sound-light, it is number-quality.

An incarnation of a being represents one of the many "film frames" arbitrarily separated from its existential unity, the *ātmā* is multidimensional. But *prājña* is a state of awareness, not a particular "place"; it is within us already, it is not outside us or foreign to us.

To comprehend one's own true nature, with all its boundless possibilities, means "to vibrate" *prājña*. If many, though on the plane of *viśva,* consciously experience the lower *taijasa* plane, few are those who truly experience higher *taijasa* and fewer still those who experience, or better still *are,* the unity of *prājña.*

Prājña is beyond the world of names and forms; it is the spiritual sphere, the state of pure knowledge because it represents the noumenon, which contains all the potentialities of being. Knowledge is not, therefore, referred to objects, and in fact one should not even speak of knowledge, but of self-knowledge or self-evidence; it is the sphere of *aseity*[1].

In the state of *prājña, ātmā* constitutes the first determination of the absolute *ātman,* just as *Brahmā* or *Īśvara* represents

[1] Underived or independent existence; property of a being that has in itself its raison d'être.

the first determination of *Brahman Nirguṇa* (non-qualified *Brahman*). In *prājña* what people normally call good-evil, small-large, etc., vanishes because every polarity, duality, opposition disappears. In *prājña* there is unity, indivisibility. It is not One-without-a-second (Fourth state) because it represents that from which the second, and therefore differentiation, irradiates. It is the geometrical point which, though without dimension, is nonetheless the first determination of a plane. *Prājña* is a spark from the principial Fire.

> «... it is this Self (*ātman*) within my heart, smaller than a grain of rice, than a grain of barley, than a seed of mustard, than a grain of millet, than the kernel of a grain of millet: this very Self which is within my heart is greater than the earth, greater than space, greater than the sky, greater than all the worlds.
>
> Foundation of all activity, of all desire, of all perceptions of smell and taste, embracing all there is; silent, indifferent is this Self within my heart. This is *Brahman* itself. He who says of himself: "Emerging from this world I shall enter *Brahman*", in truth has no doubts to be in the right».
>
> (*Chāndogya Up.*: III, XIV, 3-4)

> «In this city of *Brahman* a subtle lotus forms a dwelling, within which there is a small space. One must seek that which exists within this space, one must desire to know it».
>
> (*Chāndogya Up.*: VIII, I, 1)

VI *Sūtra of the Upaniṣad*

It (prājña) is the supreme Lord, the Omniscient, the inner Ruler, the Source of all; in it all things originate and dissolve.

Since *prājña* is the noumenon or the principial state of all possible movement, in it every thing appears and disappears, in it the states of *taijasa* and *viśva* emerge with their unlimited individual and universal expressions, and into it they return.

As the origin of all, it is omniscient because *ātmā,* on its own plane, spontaneously knows the totality of its own being; it is the inner Ruler because, although not acting, it co-ordinates and directs, with its presence alone, all the expressions of its different states; as the first determination it is, in fact, the source of all further development.

The *ātmā,* as already mentioned, may be on its own plane; it may be externalized on the twofold plane of *taijasa,* it may, furthermore, be externalized on the plane of *viśva*; to do so, it uses different sheaths, vehicles, contact tools, as we have seen in *sūtra* III and IV.

> «An eternal fragment of Myself, appeared as a living soul (*jīvabhūta*) in the world of mortals, attracts towards itself the [five] senses and the mind (*manas*), as the sixth organ, which root their foundation in *prakṛti*».
>
> «When the [internal] Lord takes a body-form, and when he abandons it, He takes these (*indriya*) with him as the wind gathers the perfumes of a place [carrying them away with it]».
>
> (*Bhagavadgītā*: XV, 7-8)

On the plane of *taijasa, ātmā,* with its powers of projection, creates of its own accord the body of contact with its corresponding life sphere; on the plane of *viśva,* on the contrary, its physical shroud is created by those representing its parents. But all this should not be viewed in absolute terms; suffice it to think that the gross-physical body is nothing but condensed energy, relatively stable, or inert mass which may dissolve into energy. Moreover, a distinction should be made between the existential planes, or systems of co-ordinates, and the being-consciousness that experiences such systems.

As we said, the three states are three vibrating existential levels upon which *ātmā* lives, moves and is.

Someone may ask: if what we said is the truth, then why do suffering and ignorance exist in this world?

First of all one must be aware of the fact that suffering is an effect, not a cause; it is the effect of the identification of the sensorial ego with a vehicle of expression and with the qualities (*guṇa*) that the vehicle expresses.

The incarnate consciousness, when it identifies with one of its expressive qualities and with a mere tool of contact, can only be reductive; its "diminution", its dwarfing, its degradation must necessarily have repercussions upon its cognitive capacity, so that it becomes a partial and limited knower. Ignorance or non-knowledge of its own nature (*avidyā*), in turn, brings suffering, conflict, alienation. To believe to be what one is not causes tension and conflict because nature strives to regain its original condition. In addition, this "lack" of being produces compensations within the world of objects, leading to the production of continuous surrogates at all levels. And this is evident: when, for any reason, one is not oneself one tries to be outside of oneself. But whatever compensation and gratification may be obtained, one can never be fulfilled, because these gratifications cannot solve the fundamental problem of existence which is that of being Unity, of resolving fragmentation and oblivion, of being, in fact, Being. Family, social, political, cultural, etc., compensations actually alienate *ātmā* even further. This is no conjecture, but a simple observation, a self-evident fact.

But why must *ātmā* or the incarnate *jīva* identify? Why is it exposed to this process of alienation? The answer is simple or complex depending on the degree of "light" one possesses.

One might begin by saying that for *ātmā* this represents *one* of its *nature's* expressive modes. And why should *ātmā* have such a nature? The empirical mind is able to discuss everything except the nature of a datum; the question cannot but lead inevitably to a *regressio ad infinitum.*

If the nature of *ātmā* were characterized only by identification it should, out of inexorable necessity, *endure* suffering and alienation. Fortunately it has another mode of being, that is to experience the levels of *viśva* and *taijasa* without, however, creating any identification, without becoming one with its emotion-feelings. It is the optimal state on the manifest plane, although experiencing, one is not bound by the fruit of the experience nor by the experience itself. This implies, in other terms, that one becomes "center" or "principle of fixity", of transcendence, transforming oneself from lunar (☽) to solar (☉) element.

When *māyā-śakti* is left to itself, it "enjoys itself"; when it is dominated and directed by the *Śiva* principle, it constitutes the "prime matter" for the creation of a *cosmos* or of Harmony.

This solar state offers neither expectations or frustrations because it lives in *freedom*; freedom from objects, from the qualities of objects and even from the propulsive forces that urge one to acquire and retain.

Those who deeply identify with their world of objects and qualities, to the point of considering themselves "matter", find it hard to grasp this state. The *Bhagavadgītā* teaches a type of action that is not imprisoning, and so does western Hermeticism.

But if this solar modality is the best, why do beings today fail to express it?

Today, in fact, many beings would prefer not to find themselves involved in identification-suffering and are trying to reject their style of life; but it must be pointed out that such awareness flashed forward *only today*; there was a time when that life style was perfectly suited to their state of consciousness.

For example, today we are *free* to drink a glass of wine and this causes no problems for us except that of enjoying an opportunity, but we are also free to identify with the wine to such an extent that one day we become alcoholics, now we are in a state of brutishness, conflict and suffering, apart from the *difficulty* of dis-identifying and moving ourselves away from drinking.

The individual, if we wish to keep to this banal example, is free to drink without creating identification and suffering, just as he is free to become dependent on and a slave to alcohol.

One can presently be the total victim of consumer goods, but this is because one wants to be.

It is obvious that to "lose oneself" in an object means alienating one's true essence or nature, which continues, nonetheless, to claim its recognition, its realization, its own freedom. Hence the conflict and the dualism that enter the being's living space. On the one hand there is the "lost", "forgotten" nature-essence which requires expression, on the other an urge towards the external world to enjoy events and things; the incarnate consciousness finds itself between two forces and feels frustrated. Dissatisfaction, which can never be sated within the world of objects, is born of the loss of true identity, and oblivion of one's deepest nature.

The solution cannot be found, therefore, in drowning or losing oneself more and more in objects, but in being able to return to one's "proper place", in being able to regain one's dignity.

Does any other way of being exist for the entity? Yes, it does, and that is, going back to our previous example, that of *not drinking* at all. This, in existential terms, implies being in *prājña,* where the *ātmā-being* rests upon itself, with itself and for itself. Here there is neither the desiring individual-subject nor the desired object because all dualism has vanished. This is the non-manifest, non-objectivating, non-exteriorising state. The being-entity discovers itself to be pure principial or causal point (*bindukāraṇa*), in bliss without objects, without ego, in *pax profunda* or Serenity (*saṁprasāda*).

If one asks whether the being has other ways of being, the answer is yes. There is yet another way which is that of resolving oneself completely in the *Parabindu, Mahābindu,* in *Brahman Nirguṇa* or in *Turīya.* At this point that being-entity with its determination and qualification dissolves, like salt in water, into the non-determined *Fourth.*

What if the *Fourth* turned out to have the nature of "emptiness", of "vacuity", of "nothingness"? There is no such thing as "nothing", precisely because it is nothing; this is simply a mental representation. The horns of a hare, Śaṅkara says, do not exist, they are not even a nothing, the non-existent is not; and a being who is cannot suddenly find himself in nothingness which is not.

The *Fourth* is the total, absolute Reality, the root of all, it is the metaphysical foundation of the Being and of the non being, of the noumenon and of the phenomenon; while the being-*bindu* is just a simple determination of this *Parabindu*, as the waters of a river, which has a form and a name, is simply a determination of the boundless ocean.

Therefore, a being may be:

- pure being on its own plane (≙)
- in a solar position (☉)
- in a lunar position (☽)

The latter condition is represented by Narcissus who, by projecting his image, falls in love with his own "shadow" and, forgetting himself, dies to his being and emerges as a... shadow.

Beings are free to suffer or rejoice, to lose or find themselves, to be or not to be. In this freedom of choice and direction, beings are the arbiters of their own destiny, the cause of their own effects, masters or slaves of their own existence.

For many westerners such a vision, though quite simple, is difficult to grasp because unconsciously they are conditioned by the concept of a manifestation *imposed* by a creator God-person and from which man can never escape, unless the God-master himself disposes otherwise.

We have spoken about three states, and in fact of four, but in reality, as already mentioned, there is but one state, that of awareness. For example, the dream state is considered as such only when the dream *is over*; as long as it lasts there is no sensation of illusion or of decreased awareness; within the dream one is conscious. Similarly, the state of dreamless sleep or deep sleep may be considered a condition of *oblivion* only when viewed from the waking state. While experiencing *suṣupti* one is fully aware, not of the objects of *viśva* and *taijasa*, but of the Self-*ātmā*. Thus, while experiencing the three states, the subject and object may or may not be there, but awareness cannot be missing; it always exists.

One is conscious during wakefulness, dream and sleep, whereby it may be concluded that consciousness is the *constant* and the sole factor common to the three states.

Prājña is the state of pure Consciousness where the Being reveals itself without any superimposition of ego-thought-emotion; *taijasa* is the state where Consciousness is veiled by subtle objects, or subtle objects are layered over pure Consciousness; *viśva* is the state where the gross object-events are superimposed on pure Consciousness.

But he who has *comprehended* knows that there is neither dreamer nor dream in the subtle state, neither dreamer nor dream in the waking state, because for him only Consciousness exists, shining of its own light not darkened by any superimposition of ego, non-ego nor by any state and movement of existence. This means he has realized the unity of the three states and, of course, all that unity may imply.

Similarly, one may be under water, on the ground or in the air, but he will constantly be aware of himself, separate from the objects of experience and from the existential states he is living through.

The coming and going (transmigration) from the state of *prājña* to the state of *viśva* and vice versa, is described in the *Bṛhadāraṇyaka Upaniṣad* (IV, III, 15 ff.).

Here begin Gauḍapāda's *kārikās*

1. Viśva (first quarter) pervades all things and experiences external (gross) objects, taijasa (second quarter) experiences the inner (subtle) ones, prājña (third quarter) experiences total consciousness (undifferentiated state): from this it may be deduced that the same entity is considered threefold.

2. Viśva knows through the right eye, taijasa through the inner organ of the mental instrument and prājña through the space (ākāśa) in the heart. Thus (jīvātman itself) appears in the body in a threefold manner.

3. Viśva enjoys the use of gross objects, taijasa from the subtle ones and prājña experiences bliss. Fruition is, therefore, threefold.

4. Viśva enjoys the gross world, taijasa the subtle one and prājña enjoys happiness. Enjoyment is, therefore, threefold.

5. He who knows the subject and the object of fruition, associated with each of the three states, is no longer afflicted by the objects (of these states) even when he experiences them.

6. It is certain that creation belongs to those beings who have a (real) existence. Thus, prāṇa manifests all objects and the principial Puruṣa creates separately the multiform rays of consciousness (jīva)[1].

7. Some thinkers consider creation as the power (of divinity), while other compare it to a mere dream or a mental projection (which a magician may perform).

8. «Creation takes place by the will of the Lord» state some, while others who consider time as real state that manifestation derives from time.

---

[1] Literally *amśu*: "Ray of light". *Jīva* is a ray of light of *ātman*.

9. Some think that the creation exists so that (the Lord) may draw enjoyment from it, while others attribute it to a simple game (of the Lord). This (act of creation) is inherent in the nature of the resplendent Being; but what desire might be supposed in one for whom all is complete?

VII *Sūtra of the Upaniṣad*

The Sages believe that the Fourth – which has knowledge neither of the internal (subjective) nor of the external (objective) world, nor simultaneously of the former and the latter, and which, ultimately, is not (even) a unity of integral consciousness, as it is neither conscious nor unconscious – is adṛṣṭa: invisible, avyavahārya: non agent, agrāhya: incomprehensible, alakṣana: indefinable, acintya: unthinkable, avyapadeśya: indescribable; it is the only pratyayasāra: essence of self knowledge, without any trace of manifestation, fullness of peace and bliss devoid of duality: it is the ātman and as such it must be known.

> «The one who has eyes, the one who is dreaming, the one who is asleep and the one who is beyond sleep: of these four different states, the fourth is the utmost.
>
> In the first three (quarters) there is a fourth of *Brahma*, and in the remaining one the other three quarters».
>
> (*Maitry Up.*: VII, 11)
>
> «Its fourth glittering *pāda* is that which shines beyond the atmosphere, *Turīya* means *caturtha*».
>
> (*Bṛhadāraṇyaka Up.*: V, XIV, 3)

This fourth state cannot be object of language, it is without comparison, it is impossible to correlate and discuss. Its reality, its evidence, may be described only in "negative" terms, in the sense that it is not something the sensorial mind can perceive or think. It should not even be considered as a "state", nor an object of experience nor a point of view; it is not even the principial Unity because this has within itself the potential of duality, in fact the *Fourth* is One-without-a-second, it is pure act, not mixed with any potentiality, it is the Infinite in its true sense. The mind (*manas*) could vacillate faced with this Reality which allows no image to relate with.

The ontological One is the trunk from which the branches and fruit stem, but the *Fourth* represents the invisible root, both transcendent and immanent. One might say that manifestation or the threefold nature "appears" upon this screen, which represents the *constant*, absolute and without a second. «*Turīya* is the all-pervading source of all beings»[1], comments Śaṅkara. The preceding OM (VI *Sūtra*) is assimilated to *Brahman Saguṇa*; this *Fourth* is *Brahman Nirguṇa*, the without sound, *aśabda*.

> «In him who is without parts, beyond action, of whom nothing may be said, immaculate, sublime bridge towards immortality, equal to the fire that has burnt up all fuel».
>
> (*Śvetāśvatara Up.*: VI, 19)

---

[1] The numerous passages in inverted commas along with the text, unless otherwise specified, are quoted from *Śaṅkara*'s commentary in: *Māṇḍūkya Upaniṣad with Gauḍapāda's kārikā and Śaṅkara's commentary*, with notes by Raphael. Edizioni Āśram Vidyā, Rome, Italy. (Italian edition).

Gauḍapāda's *kārikās*

10. *In the immutable non-dual and supreme Lord all suffering ends. This resplendent Turīya is considered the all-pervading source of all entities.*

Duality, at whatever level or degree, produces tension and conflict because the being, on the plane of multiplicity, is lacking, is imperfect, is alienated, is oblivious.

To realize *Turīya* means finding again one's proper place, integral completeness; it means innocent unveiling of the essence, therefore it does not mean unveiling *my* note or *yours* or second nature, but it implies unveiling Fullness.

Turīya is the sole reality where all suffering caused by alienation dissolves, together with those particular experiences belonging to that determined manifestation.

11. *Viśva and taijasa are conditioned by cause and effect; prājña is conditioned by cause. But in Turīya there is neither cause nor effect.*

If *prājña* represents the germ, the seed or the cause of production, then *taijasa* and *viśva,* who are its developments, represent the effects, subtle for the former, gross for the latter.

Now, to resolve the effect (either subtle or gross) the prime cause or the principial state must first be removed. In *prājña* the being, as seen previously, rests in itself, with itself and for itself, it is illuminated by its own light because it has resolved in its true unity, which is principial Unity. It perceives no duality, nothing that is external to itself as the Being or different from itself. Its veil, or superimposition, is made up only by primordial *avidyā,* or by that limitation that is inherent to the nature of all "determinations". *Prājña* is the first determination, the qualified Being (*Saguṇa*), therefore it has in itself the nature of the appearing and of the disappearing.

Seen from the metaphysical perspective, *prājña* is a limitation, a specificity, it is *tamas*-obscurity, it is an indication, a definition; and some beings, ripened out of their *karma,* wish to leave it altogether.

Turīya is beyond time, space and cause. *Turīya* is its own cause, it is the cause of causes, or the non-caused, therefore without origin or end; *Turīya* is the infinite Possibility of all causal determinations, while *prājña* represents only *one* determined potentiality. The geometrical point, although without dimensions, can manifest only lines, planes and volumes, thus it is a point already determined, qualified, specific in its nature.

The mind cannot grasp anything greater than the geometrical or universal point, therefore if the being were to be defined as mind-thought alone it could not know the *Fourth,* the Infinite, the non-Qualified, because it would not be able to ideate or to perceive what is beyond the reach of thought.

12. Prājña knows neither the self nor the non-self, neither truth nor error, but Turīya, being the eternal and universal Witness, comprehends all.

13. The absence of duality is common both to prājña and Turīya. But prājña is associated with sleep-seed (bīja-nidrā) while sleep does not exist in Turīya.

It is necessary to pay attention in order not to confuse the non-duality of *Turīya* with the unity of *prājña*. In other words, one must distinguish between the ontological sphere (of the principial or mathematical One) and the purely metaphysical sphere. The One is the *beginning* of a determined series, therefore of multiplicity, and this is *prājña*. *Turīya* is authentic non-duality because it is without beginning, principle, or unity meant as the origin of a series. Therefore, *Turīya* is beyond number. To say one is the same as saying two, three and so on, but saying non-two means leaving numbering, quantity and quality altogether behind, it means affirming the absolute Unity which does not imply any series whatsoever.

Non-duality is the culmination of all monotheistic, dualistic and pluralistic religious or philosophical conceptions.

From the state of *prājña* one returns to the plane of individual or universal manifestation, depending on the degree of realization attained, but from *Turīya* there is no return. And this *Upaniṣad* with Gauḍapāda's *kārikās*, expresses precisely this Reality without birth (*Ājāti*).

14. The first two (viśva and taijasa) are associated with the condition of dream and sleep respectively; prājña with the condition of dreamless sleep, but in Turīya the knowers see neither dream nor sleep.

15. Dream applies to wrong perception and sleep to ignoring reality. When these two factors are removed the state of Turīya is attained.

If dream-waking is characteristic of *viśva*, dreaming of *taijasa*, and deep sleep of *prājña, Turīya* lies beyond these three conditions, though containing them. In the subtle and gross states perception is faulty because one is guided by feelings, by mental representations or by sensorial opinion. An individual does not perceive, for example, a true tree or vase, but the image he conjures up of the vase or tree, wherefore the truth in itself, or the "thing in itself" remains unknown. With our sensorial mind we always perceive phenomena, fluctuating in the world of becoming. A Phenomenon is a "second", it is other than Being, because is less than Being.

Sensorial knowledge, according to contemporary psychology, occurs because the five senses transfer to the mind (the sixth sense) all the data of an object that they detect and perceive; the mind, in turn, elaborates the data and, by means of analysis, deduction, induction, memory, etc., formulates a *concept* of the object. This demonstrates that this kind of knowledge occurs through mental structures which are "fictions". It is the knowledge of the "as if". Therefore, it is knowledge of concepts; but a concept is not the authentic *truth* about something, it is simply its representation, a fictitious reconstruction. In addition, a concept is always referred to something, so that we have the following triplicity: the knowing subject, the mind-concept, the conceptual object of knowledge.

This triplicity, however, excludes true knowledge of what Unity-Being is; wherefore, conceptual knowledge refers only to phenomena that are other from self, and to the laws which govern these phenomena. If the reality-being is not split from Being-Reality, then knowledge cannot be *a posteriori* because this knowledge would imply distinction, separation and duality.

In *prājña* Being knows directly, and not in a fictitious way, to be the prime cause, but it does not know yet the ultimate Reality of Non-Being or absolute and non-conditioned Being. It is this ignorance-oblivion (*avidyā*) of one's true absolute nature which causes wandering within the spheres of *taijasa* and *viśva*. *Viśva* and *taijasa* are simple "film frames" of the *prājña*-Idea and even *prājña*-Idea itself is one of the *infinite* "film frames" of the absolute *Brahman*.

16. *When the sleeping jīva, under the influence of māyā without origin, awakens from its sleep, it realizes That which is without birth, duality, dream and sleep.*

17. *If the phenomenal world had any existence whatsoever, then it would cease to exist, but this multiplicity, which is māyā, is nothing other than non-duality, which is the sole reality.*

If realization-knowledge of non-duality is obtained after the dissolution of the phenomenal world, how can one, we might ask, resolve oneself in *Turīya* if the world still exists?

If the multiple world of names and forms were absolute reality, not only would it not allow the notion of Unity and Non-duality, but it would also condition the Absolute which, to be such, may not be conditioned by the relative, just as the noumenon may not be conditioned by the phenomenon. The world of names and forms are simply lights and shadows projected on the screen of *Turīya*, and, as it is pure contingency, it may be interrupted at any moment.

The gross, subtle and causal phenomenal universe is a continuity-discontinuity that may be dissolved whenever one decides to do so. A non-reality cannot invalidate absolute Reality, just like an error, which is contingent, cannot invalidate Truth that is eternal. Error, compared to truth, is a non-being which can be resolved, and this is evident at any moment; once resolved it vanishes completely, it no longer exists. To look for the error or *māyā*, once the truth has been recognized, is like looking for the footprints of a bird in the air.

18. *Distinctive knowledge ceases insofar as imagined by a particular being. This explanation aims at facilitating the teaching: duality ceases to exist when realization is attained.*

VIII *Sūtra of the Upaniṣad*

This is the sole ātman (described previously as having four quarters) whose nature, from the syllables point of view, is identical with OM. The word OM, composed of parts is now examined for what regards the sounds (or letters: mātrās). Thus the quarters are identical with the syllables (the parts) and the syllables with the quarters. The syllables are: A. U. M.

IX *Sūtra of the Upaniṣad*

Vaiśvānara, whose sphere (of activity) is the waking state, is designated by the letter A, which is the first measure and that which pervades all. He who knows this attains all desirable things and becomes the first.

X *Sūtra of the Upaniṣad*

Taijasa, whose sphere (of activity) is the state of dream, is designated by the letter U, which is the second measure (of AUM) due to its superiority and its intermediate position. He who knows this acquires superior knowledge and realizes harmony with the whole. Not one of his descendants will ignore Brahman.

XI *Sūtra of the Upaniṣad*

Prājña, whose sphere (of activity) is the state of deep sleep is designated by the letter M, which is the third measure (of AUM) and is also that in which everything dissolves. He who thus knows is able to measure all (the threefold world) and becomes the point of absorption.

Gauḍapāda's *kārikās*

19. When one comprehends the identity of viśva with the letter A, the characteristic of being first and all-pervading is also reached.

20. When one comprehends the identity of taijasa with the letter U, there clearly unveils utkarṣaḥ: the superiority of the subtle and of the intermediate state (of U in relation to A and M, and of taijasa with reference to viśva and prājña) over the gross.

21. When the identity of prājña with the letter M is compreheded, māna (measure of knowledge of the worlds) and laya, reabsorbtion, clearly unveils.

22. He who, without hesitation, grasps the similarity between the three states is a great sage, greeted and venerated by all beings.

23. The letter A leads to viśva, the letter U to taijasa and the letter M to prājña. But in amātra (not measurable in that not subject to experience) nothing remains to be attained.

These last *kārikās* disclose the identification of the three letters or sounds (AUM) with the three states. *Turīya* corresponds to the soundless OM or to the absence of manifested sound.

Śaṅkara writes in his comment to this *kārikā*: «And finally, the sound M leads to *prājña*; but when, in turn, the sound M fades away, causality itself is surpassed, wherefore nothing remains to be accomplished».

So we comprehend that the development of bodily individuality occurs in *viśva*, extensive development of the formal and non-formal extra-corporeal states occurs in *taijasa*, supra-individual and principial development occurs in *prājña*, finally, supreme realization or integral liberation from the formal, the non-formal universal and the principial manifestation occurs in *Turīya*.

XII *Sūtra of the Upaniṣad*

The AUM devoid of parts (and of letters), which cannot be seized (by the senses), extinct of all appearances[1], *full bliss and non-dual, is Turīya. Thus AUM is undoubtedly the Self. He who knows this immerses the self (microcosm) in the Self (Brahman).*

The AUM[2] as pure essence of sound is ungraspable by the sensorial beings, also because its realization implies no longer perceiving *appearance, vision*, duality. It is non-qualified (*Nirguṇa*), non-determined OM. Gauḍapāda says: «He who knows the OM without measure is blessed and free of duality. He who knows OM is the true sage, nobody else». OM, *Fourth*, *Turīya*, *Brahman Nirguṇa* are equivalent terms.

The realization of *Turīya* is the true aim of the metaphysical *yoga*-pathway. If the word metaphysical means "beyond the physical", and the term physical means "nature-substance", then the metaphysical vision goes beyond the natured[3] and the naturing[4] (created and creative nature). To speak, for example,

---

[1] *Prapañcopāsana*; that has no development of manifestation.

[2] AUM devoid of parts, (*a-mātra*), without measure, and metaphysical foundation of the primordial sound.

[3] *Natura naturata*, Lat.: created by or in nature

[4] *Natura naturans*, Lat.: active, creative process of nature; causal agent.

of *taijasa* in metaphysical terms, as it often happens, is not appropriate because *taijasa* is as substantial and "material" as the *viśva* sphere, the only difference between them is in degrees of "density", and therefore of vibration, as Gauḍapāda demonstrates in the second chapter of the text. *Prājña* is the noumenal sphere, but the noumenon is a polar aspect of the phenomenon and both are found upon the plane of the manifest, whether gross or germinal is of little importance. One may say that the three represent, respectively, the spiritual state (*prājña*), the psychic (*taijasa*) and the gross-material one (*viśva*). The metaphysical *Turīya* transcends these states although it bestows upon them life and chance to develop.

Generally, these states are named: gross, subtle and causal, which corresponds perfectly to what we mean.

Gauḍapāda's *kārikās*

24. OM must be known quarter by quarter because the quarters are identical to the letters (sounds). Once one has grasped (the significance) of OM, quarter by quarter, one must no longer think of anything else.

25. The mind must be in identity with OM because OM is Brahman free of fear. The being absorbed in OM is relieved of all sense of dread.

When one comprehends the spirit of OM quarter by quarter, the mind must stop so that consciousness may realize the state of *avasthātraya-sākṣin* (witness of the three states). This involves being a universal Witness and having free access to the entire "dimension" of Being; it implies realizing Unity of Being and not of a mere state, much less one belonging to the earthly system of co-ordinates. We cannot but grasp its profound implications and the enormous realizative possibilities.

26. Praṇava OM is certainly the non-supreme Brahman and also the supreme Brahman. OM is without cause, without effect, without interior and exterior, it is imperishable.

Śaṅkara comments: «OM is at once the non-supreme (*apara*) and the supreme (*para*) *Brahman.* When, from the point of view of the ultimate truth, sounds and quarters merge (in OM without sound), OM becomes perfectly identical to the supreme *Brahman.* That is why it is said to be without cause, without a second because nothing exists that is different from it and also because nothing exists outside of it; nor is it linked to any effect; therefore, it is without cause and dwells within and outside of all things; it is also free of birth... ».

The two *Brahman* (*apara* and *para*) are not two different and opposite Beings (duality); the non-supreme *Brahman* or *Saguṇa* (qualified) is a simple reflection or determination of the supreme transcendent *Brahman* or *Nirguṇa* (non-qualified). If one wishes to see things from the point of view of the ultimate truth, the supreme Reality is represented only by *Brahman Nirguṇa,* because *Brahman Saguṇa* is simply fleeting and determined; to take the relative for the absolute, the phenomenon for the noumenon, the fleeting for the constant, means to be under the sway of *avidyā.*

27. Praṇava OM is, in truth, the beginning, the intermediate stage and the end of all things. Knowing praṇava thus one achieves identity at once.

28. One must comprehend that praṇava OM is Īśvara who dwells in the hearts of everyone. By meditating upon the all-pervading OM the intelligent person ceases to suffer.

OM is the beginning, the middle and the end; all things appear and vanish in It. It is the substratum of all beings. It is all-pervading and dwells in the hearts of everyone. *Īśvara* is also the immanent Principle, and the multiple world of names and forms has this common denominator; it has, as its foundation, this principial unity.

Through identity with the Principle, that informs all, one realizes the unity of life; human consciousness is no longer individual, but becomes universal[1]. Similarly, although the body has various organs and limbs, the human individual feels one and indivisible.

The multiplicity of life depends on the Īśvara-Principle, just as the latter depends on the absolute Brahman.

The non-realized ones see with the eye of duality because they perceive only form and volumes that are different, separate and unmatched betweent them, but the realized ones have the privilege of seeing life in terms of unity, of synthesis. For the realized ones the three states are not three but one.

A dualistic philosophical vision leads to conflict, to competition, to struggle, to solipsistic individualism, arrogance and war, while the philosophical vision of Unity leads to the awareness that behind the illusionary screen of differentiation there lies a sole nature, a sole homeland, a sole Principle.

29. He who recognizes the measureless OM is blessed and free from duality. He who knows OM is a true sage, and no one else.

---

[1] This represents the realization of *savikalpa samādhi*.

Śaṅkara comments: «beyond all measure (*amātraḥ*) is *Turīya*. In fact *mātrā* means measure, and what has no measure or is unlimited vastness is called *anantamātraḥ*, as nobody may determine its size or measure. Again, it is bliss because it is non-dual. Only he who knows OM, according to the foregoing explanation, and nobody else, however learned in the scriptures, is a true *Muni* (silent one) as he has realized the supreme Reality».

If Being-*Iśvara* is the measure of all manifest things, *Turīya* is beyond all measure because it transcends every determination of time, space and cause. But, on the other hand, one must not think that *Turīya* represents chaos out of which a cosmos may develop thanks to the action of a demiurge. Chaos, instead, is represented by *prakṛti* or the "primordial Waters".

Some people, who identify with individuality or with the mere aspect of the demiurge, speak of *Turīya*, and therefore of the metaphysical level, as "losing oneself in the infinite", as they consider the infinite as something indefinite formless and chaotic, a disorderly and uncontrolled power. All this does not belong to the Infinite but to the collective unconscious, or rather, to the collective subconscious. So they try to prove that Reality must be characterized by a precise limit and outline, by a precise determined and qualified physiognomy. They maintain that to emerge from the undetermined in order for the individuality to appear is the precise task of the being. They thus confuse the undetermined collective unconscious or *prakṛti* with the metaphysical Infinite, which, by its very nature, expresses the negation of all limits, determinations and qualifications.

Turīya is considered by some as a "negative" state, in the ordinary sense of the term, so the position of these people, who are identified with the "positive" polarity, is absurd when they affirm that the state of *Turīya* should be refuted because it contains negativity. Apart from other considerations, don't they realize that negative-positive, movement-stasis, being-non being, definite-indefinite, determined-undetermined, etc., are terms of comparison that just the empirical mind can conceive?

Gauḍapāda will say later on that some aspirant *yogis* are afraid of this metaphysical realization because they believe they will lose their individuality, awareness of themselves as separate and determined beings.

At this point someone might think that the *Upaniṣad* proposes a simple "description" of the states of Being as a show of erudition and believe that Gauḍapāda and Śaṅkara, the two greatest *realizers* and codifiers of the *Advaita Vedānta*, wrote their commentaries for purely cultural reasons. But that is not so. Culture, as it is conceived in the West, may even stray one from the true meaning or "spirit" of a Tradition. Not only that. To intellectually understand a theory or doctrine to the point of being top of the class or a knowledgeable "wise guy", just because one is provided with a good memory and mental ability, is of little use for realizative purposes.

To have a knowledge apparently comparable to that of a Master does not mean being a Master. A Master is a "state of consciousness"; to have realized a "Dignity" that no manasic erudition can give.

An *Upaniṣad* indicates a state of consciousness that is up to the disciple to realize. On the other hand, one may reach this state without ever having known the *Upaniṣad*. Rāmaṇa Mahāṛṣi, after a specific experience, "comprehended" the oneness of Reality, which he later found expounded in *Advaita Vedānta*.

If this *Māṇḍūkya Upaniṣad*, which is the quintessence of *Vedānta*, proposes the *mantra* AUM this is because between AUM and the states of Being, and between the universal Being and the individual one, there are precise correspondences.

Human beings are endowed with seven major *cakras*, situated along the spine and within the prāṇic or hyperphysical body, but three are the essentially important *cakras*. Now, to resonate the *mantra* within these three *cakras* means causing them to open and to allow consciousness to vibrate in unison with the universal.

When Gauḍapāda, in *kārikā* 23, holds that the letter A leads to *viśva*, the letter U to *taijasa*, and the letter M to *prājña*, it must not be taken as a figure of speech or as an intellectual conjecture.

The *cakras* are the centers of consciousness of the world of manifestation with its gross and subtle bodies, which derive from their causal body, and its three planes of consciousness: waking, dreaming, and dreamless sleep.

If one knows the *mūlādhāra cakra* to contain the fire which feeds the "earth" or the gross body (*Brahmā*); the *anāhata cakra* to be the seat of the *jīvātman* in his subtle body (*Viṣṇu*), governor of the first three *cakras*, starting with the *mūlādhāra cakra*; the *ājñā cakra* to be the seat of *ātmā* joined with *prakṛti* in the causal form of the *praṇava* OM (*Śiva*), then one may comprehend that the three states mentioned in the *Upaniṣad* are precise states of consciousness that must be realized, by opening the three access doors.

There are various types of *yogas*, or doctrines, that show the way to realize the three states, but their aim is to reach *savikalpa samādhi*, or the undivided state of *prājña-Īśvara*.

Thus, in alchemical terms, these three states and *cakras* represent salt (⊖) or Formal fire, Mercury (☿) or Mercurial fire and Sulfur (🜍) or incorruptible Fire.

We might also speak of individualized Fire, radiant Fire and noumenal Fire. (It is to be noted that Gauḍapāda entitled the fourth chapter of his *kārikā*: "On the extinction of the burning ember").

The realizational progression in alchemy is:

1. Rectification of ⊖
2. Separation of ☿ from ⊖
3. Fixing of 🜍, or solution of ☿ in 🜍.

It is not possible, here, to develop adequately these sequences (black, red, white *opus*)[1] but those who, especially westerners, comprehend them, may realize *prājña*, the One which penetrates all, by remembering that: «Fire is generated and nourished by Fire and is the child of Fire, therefore it is necessary to return to Fire so as not to fear Fire». (Flamel).

The *Asparśavāda* is the acme of every kind of ascesis, and it leads to *nirvikalpa samādhi* or to the state of *Nirguṇa*, the non-differentiated state of *Brahman* (Fourth state).

Asparśa is the pure metaphysical *yoga*, and to follow it one must have a *mens informalis*[2] because a mind conditioned by time-space-cause may conceive only the Principle or mathematical One. *Jñāna* is knowledge, but this knowledge has nothing to do with phenomena, as seen before, not even with the noumenon, but with the absolute Constant. It is a knowledge by identity because it does not operate on the subject-object relationship; it is "prime knowledge" that does not belong to the conceptual and imaginative *manas*-mind, but to the non-dual Consciousness.

Immediate awareness of *Turīya*, by means of *jñāna*, leads to Liberation (from metaphysical Ignorance) in this very life, so that the state of *jīvanmukta*, living Liberated one, is realized. This represents the indication and the purpose of this *Upaniṣad* and Gauḍapāda develops and deepens its themes.

---

[1] See, Raphael: *The Threefold Pathway of Fire*, Aurea Vidyā, New York, and, *The Pathway of Fire*, Initiation to the Kabbalah, S. Weiser, Maine, U.S.A.

[2] Non-formal higher intellect, discerning intuition, *buddhi*.

Chapter II

Vaitathya Prakaraṇa

(On the absolute non-reality of empirical experience)

1. *The Wise affirm the non-reality of object-events seen in the dream condition, both because they are situated within (the sleeping subject) and because they are circumscribed in space.*

In the first chapter, non-duality was examined with reference to the *Śruti* (non-human Tradition), in the second and subsequent chapters Gauḍapāda wishes to prove non-duality by resorting to pure reason, so as to meet the needs of those who are mainly polarized in the intellect.

At this point, we should clarify that: for *Advaita* the term non-real is not intended in the absolute sense of non-existent. For example, when we say that the objective world is unreal this does not mean that the world is non-existent like «the horns of a hare» (as Śaṅkara comments), but that it is not real when compared to the absolute Reality. The objective world is, therefore, a relative effect-phenomenon that is born, grows and dies. The transitory nature of manifestation is also shown by empirical evidence.

When asked: what is Real? *Asparśavāda* answers: Real is all that is beyond time, space and cause. Whatever falls within this threefold aspect of time, space and cause is moving, changing, contingent, a phenomenon that appears and disappears. This being so, what is beyond these categories must be *constant*, always identical to itself, without contradiction, without birth (*ajāti*, from which stems *ajātivāda*, another name for the *yoga* Gauḍapāda expounds in this book), non-determined; therefore infinite.

2. *Because of the lack of time it is impossible for the sleeper to experience something by going on the place (of the event); in fact, when he awakens he does not find himself in the place (of that event).*

3. *Furthermore, the non-reality of a chariot, etc., (perceived in a dream) is interpreted by the Śruti from the point of view of reasoning. It is said, therefore, that the false appearance of dreams, demonstrated through reasoning, is confirmed by the Śruti itself.*

4. *Just as the objects of dreams are non-real, so for the same reason, the objects perceived during the waking state are non-real. The difference (between dreaming and waking) is that (in a dream), space is limited and the objects exist inside the body.*

5. *Because of the identity of perception, recognized by inference, the wise say that the states of dreaming and waking are of the same nature.*

The question is the following: generally it is held that while the waking state is real, the dreaming one is unreal. But one might ask: what is this statement based on? The answer is: on the evidence of perception and on conscious perception itself.

Gauḍapāda, however, demonstrates that the evidence of perception and even perception in both the waking and dreaming states are identical, therefore they must be of the same nature.

6. *That which is non-real at the beginning and at the end must, necessarily, be not real in between. Although the objects (of the waking state) are of the same unreal nature (as those of the dream state), they are, nonetheless, considered real.*

This *kārikā* emphasizes the evidence of perception: these objects have an evident birth, growth, maturity and end, both in the waking and dreaming condition.

Although the objects both in the waking and dreaming state have an origin and an end, nonetheless those belonging to the waking state are considered real, while both should be considered unreal.

One might object that, although they show the same features, the objects of the waking state have a specific aim, they serve legitimate and rational purposes: they quench thirst and hunger, for example; a chair has a specific use, etc.

7. *Their utility is contradicted by the dream state. Therefore, seeing that all (the objects of waking and dreaming) have a beginning and an end, they are rightly considered not real.*

8. *The objects (perceived by the dreamer), which are rarely encountered (in the waking state) owe their existence to the (particular) conditions in which the perceiving subject exercises its mental activity, as it may happen with the dwellers of the heavens. The dreamer experiences such objects like*

a well-informed individual experiences the objects of the (waking) world.

Even in dreams the objects serve certain purposes: so we use a chair to sit and satisfy our hunger with pleasant food.

In addition, the purpose of objects belonging to the waking state is not absolute because something in the waking state may be contradicted in dreams and vice versa: the wealth one possesses in the waking state, for example, may not be transferred into the dream state.

One might object that dream objects are often deformed, grotesque, etc., while those belonging to the waking state are normal and rational.

Also this truth is not absolute, because, even in the waking state one may encounter grotesque and unexpected forms that may be bewildering the observer. Further, this objection is not valid because we should acknowledge the fact that every mode of life has its own specific characteristics, its distinctive features that may, obviously, differ from those of another way of life.

A traveler who, in the waking state, visits another country, may encounter objects he never saw before, or whose features are different from those in one's own country; the behavior of one people may be considered as absurd by another and so on.

9. *In the dream state, what is perceived by the mind as subjective is non-real, and what is perceived as objective is held to be real. But, both the object-events perceived are non-real.*

10. *In the waking state, what is imagined as subjective by the mind is non-real, and what is experienced as objective is real. But, both the object-events perceived are non-real.*

Having confuted the thesis whereby the objects perceived in the waking and dreaming states are different, Gauḍapāda now goes on to analyze what the subject perceives.

During the waking state perception is characterized by a perceiver and by a perceived object; but even in dreaming there is a subject who perceives and an object that is perceived. And just as in the waking state an object may cause pain and joy to the perceiving subject, so in the dream state there are objects which cause the perceiving subject pain or happiness too. And again, just as in wakefulness what is objective is considered to be real and what is subjective is believed to be unreal, so too, in dreaming, what is objective is held to be real, while what is subjective is considered unreal.

One might object that dreams are the dreamer's private affair and only concern him, while the waking state is a general condition involving other people.

The answer is that even in dreams the dreamer is not alone, because others are involved, just as in wakefulness. In dreams, for example, one may be teaching one's pupils, addressing a crowd, talking to members of one's family, participating in and experiencing group activities and so on.

One might again object that dream is just a recollection of the waking state, a simple appendix of it.

The answer is: although this can be true, nevertheless it is not so absolutely. In dream one experiences things and events that do not occur in the waking state. In addition, while dreaming one may have intuitions that are, even, the completion of the waking experiences. Such cases are self-evident. And when a dream experience manages to influence and modify the waking state it may no longer be considered as an illusion: an illusion produces no event, it does not determine a behavior or choice, it solves no problems.

It could be said that perception in the waking state is characterized by an intelligent continuity of thought patterns and by an intelligent production of goods to benefit waking entities.

One can reply that perception in the dream state is equally consistent, responding to the needs of that state; specifically, it should be considered that the dreaming entity experiences various clusters of events, each following its own basic theme. Furthermore, the dreaming entity, as it is clear, produces all that is needed for that experience.

In the end, one may ask: from what point of view can we affirm that dream is not real?

The above objections show that dreams are analyzed from the point of view of waking and by the thought system of this state. But, is it possible to judge a system of co-ordinates from the exclusive perspective of another system? Is it rational to hold that a three-dimensional world is dream-illusion because it cannot be perceived from a two-dimensional point of view?

Undisputed rationality and rigorous deductive logic are nevertheless related to a specific thought system in all circumstances; it follows that they cannot respond to and comprehend a different thought system.

A thought system always acts within the framework of a closed circumference, and should its premises fail its conclusions would collapse. For example, a thought system, or a point of view holds that reality may be perceived only through the senses. It is obvious that if we "identify" with such a current of thought we make it absolute, wherefore all other possible thought systems postulating different points of view are excluded *a priori*. Later Gauḍapāda indicates how the one Reality is seen in different ways by the manifold points of view of beings, so that every one considers valid his own premise and conclusion.

For *Asparśavāda* there are relative truths or "degrees of truth" which are, in fact, the expression of the various perspectives of beings, but they are all annulled in the supreme Reality.

From this point of view one can say that the materialistic ideology can be considered nihilistic, absolutist and, strangely enough, *a priori*, that it can itself to be dogmatic religion, while *Advaita* is flexible and allows for many possibilities. *Advaita,* in fact, when it moves upon the plane of relativity, does not offer absolute truths, does not deny dualism nor monism nor even materialistic phenomenalism, but considers them as "possible points of view" that contain degrees of truth.

11. *If all the objects perceived in the two states (waking and dreaming) are not real, who, then, knows these objects? Who is their creator?*

12. *The self-resplendent ātman, with the powers of its own māyā, appears as object. Only the Self is the support of the knowledge of objects; such is the conclusion of Vedānta.*

13. *When the mind, supported by the Lord (ātman), directs itself outwardly, it imagines the multiplicity of objects (such as sound, etc.) which already exist within it (in the guise of vāsanā or saṁkalpa). When it goes inward it imagines within itself different ideas (as internal objects).*

If the objects perceived in the two worlds (waking and dreaming or *viśva* and *taijasa*) are not absolutely real, in fact they are born and die, who is their creator and who is the perceiving subject?

The creator of objects, like the perceiver himself, is the *jīvātman*. The support, the foundation of this polarity, of this subject-object duality, is the *ātman*. The *ātman* is the source or root of all, without it nothing could exist either in the causal, subtle or gross states.

The first *sūtra* of the *Dṛgdṛśyaviveka* says: «An object-form is perceived, but it is the eye that perceives. This is perceived by the mind which becomes the perceiving subject. Then, the mind, with its modifications, is perceived by the Thinker-Spectator who cannot be the object of perception»[1].

This allows us to comprehend how object and subject are perceived by the ultimate Witness who, in fact, is behind this antinomy. In other words, one may speak of duality because there is an entity that affirms it. Every duality implies a third factor, which represents its synthesis and conclusion.

The *ātman*, therefore, irradiates a ray of consciousness, which represents the *jīva* (cp. *kārikā* 16) and, in turn, the *jīva*, urged by the *vāsanās*, projects the multiplicity of objects into the *taijasa* and *viśva* states with its vehicle of expression, the *manas*.

14. *The objects that are perceived as internal for the duration of the thought and the others perceived by the senses on the outside, that are referred to two points of the duration, are simply mental modifications; there is no other factor that allows their differentiation.*

15. *(Both) the objects which exist inside the mind (as subjective ones) and which are designated to be not objectively visible, and those which, objectively visible, exist on the*

---

[1] Raphael, *Self and Non-Self*, the *Dṛgdṛśyaviveka* attributed to Śaṁkara, Kegan Paul International Limited, London.

outside, are simply mental representations; the only difference lies in the different perceiving organs.

16. *First the jīva is imagined and, then, the different internal and external objects. From the impressions aroused by memory, (the jīva) acquires the corresponding knowledge.*

Are external objects, state of *Virāṭ*, projections of the individual *jīva*? No. They are projections of *Īśvara*, which is the universal *jīva*. An objective datum, or a subjective one, is simply an *idea* of the individual or of the universal thinker. A vase is simply an image-idea that a demiurge has made either gross-objective upon the *viśva* or *Virāṭ* plane, or subjective, better still *subtle*, upon the *taijasa* or *Hiraṇyagarbha* plane.

The universe is a projection of the *Māhāt* (great Mind) with various degrees of condensation (causal, subtle, gross). But the mind is only a creative, *form giving*, imaginative tool.

17. *Just like a rope, whose nature has not been well ascertained, is imagined in darkness to be a snake, a trickle of water, etc., so ātman is imagined (in various ways).*

18. *When the true nature of the rope has been ascertained, all imaginings superimposed (onto the rope) vanish and nothing else remains but the rope. This occurs with the ātman as well.*

19. *The ātman is imagined as prāṇa and as other indefinite things. This is due to the māyā of the resplendent (ātman) through which it unveils.*

What is the relationship between the *jīva* and the world of objects?

At this point it would be useful to go back to what was said previously, particularly in the note to the VI *Sūtra* of the *Upaniṣad*.

Now we can provide a summary table concerning the planes of existence and the constitution of the individual being, to have a better comprehension of the whole. Furthermore, to show that this threefold division, plus the Fourth, which is metaphysical, is not unique to *Advaita*, we also provide an outline of the states of Being according to other branches of the Tradition.

Existential planes:

Ātman-Brahman

Individual	Universal
Prājña	*Īśvara*
Taijasa	*Hiraṇyagarbha*
Viśva	*Virāṭ*

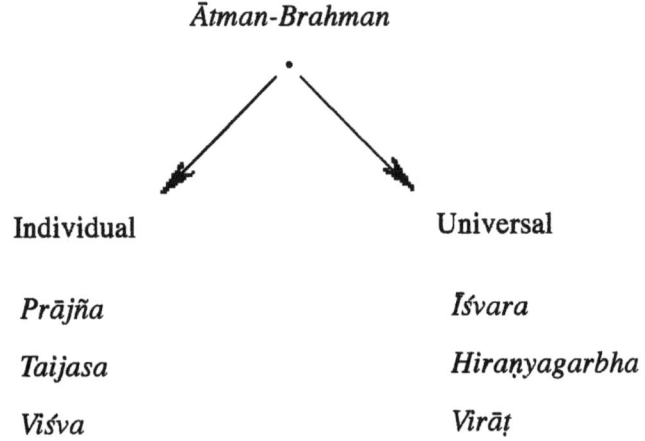

Constitution of a being:

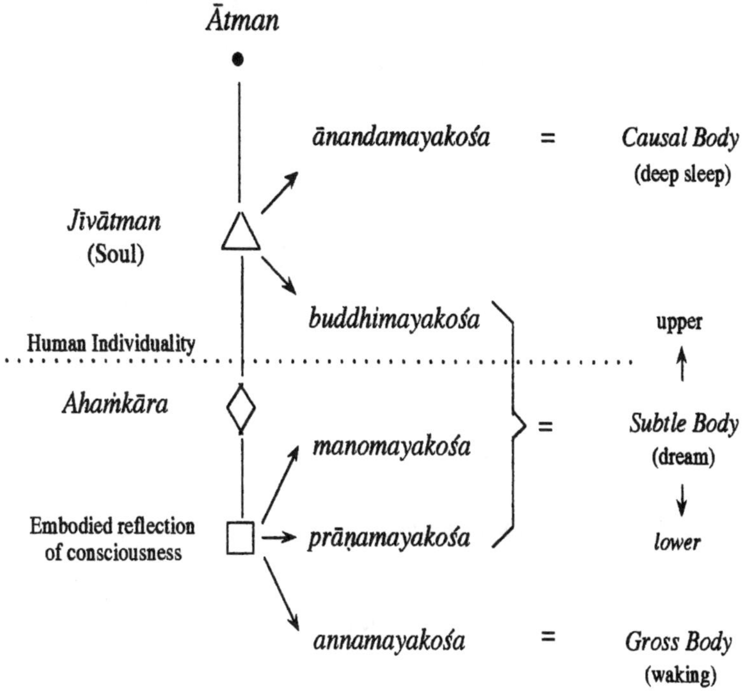

The first three sheaths, from the bottom up, are shared with animals (even animals have a rudimental *manas*, although this is the fundamental feature of the human being). The other two sheaths are shared with the world of the... "Gods".

Although sustaining and nourishing it, the *ātman* transcends manifestation.

According to the *Tao* Tradition this is the picture:

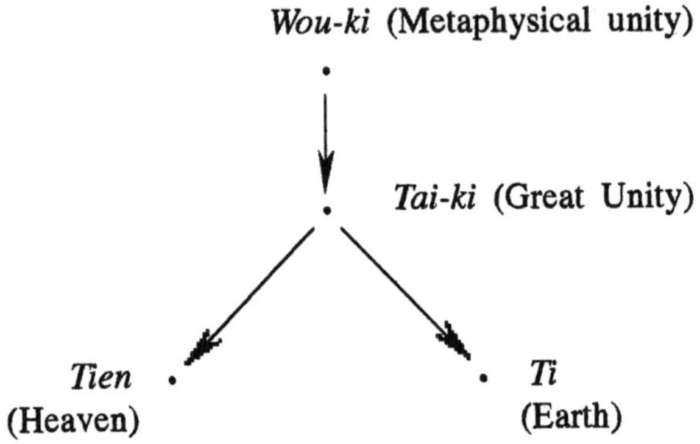

According to *Qabbālāh*:

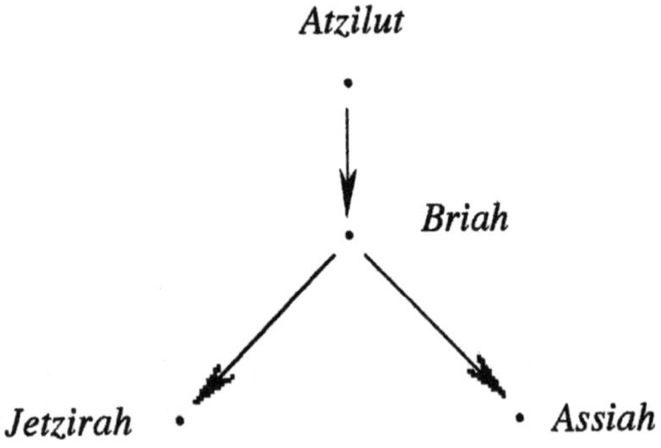

According to Buddhism:

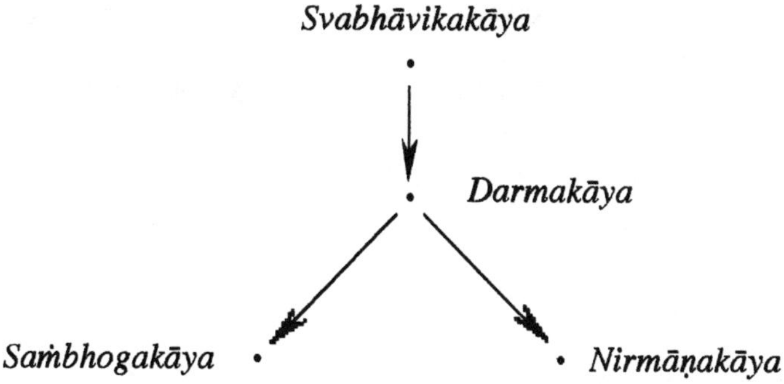

According to Greek Tradition as synthesized by Plotinus:

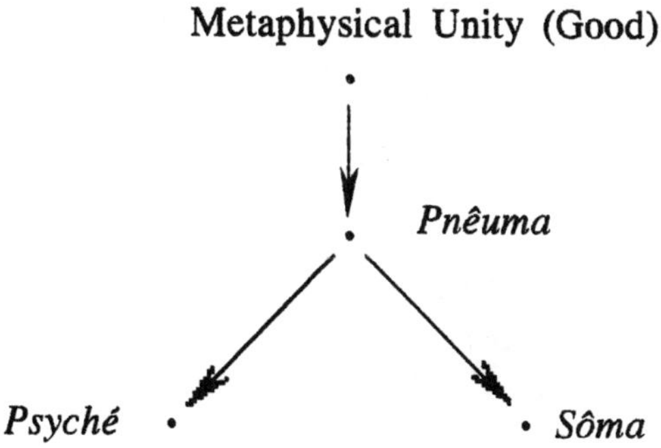

The individual, by identifying with the external world and with his projections, believes that these things represent the Self, the ultimate reality; and as the representations are many, constantly changing, one is obliged to embrace many truths in time-space.

So *ātman* or the supreme Reality, appears in one's eyes now as a particular thing, now as another.

The example of the rope and the snake, or others, is typical of the *Vedānta* teaching. The rope is imagined to be a snake, a stick, a garland, a trickle of water, etc., according to the perspective taken by the observer (the various thought systems).

This allows one to see how many different points of view there may be, although they all try to point to that one unchanging Reality. The materialist identifies the supreme Reality with "matter", the idealist with the idea, the mental-manasic with thought, the spiritualist with the spirit, the theist with the God person, and so on according to the perspective the *manas* is capable of conceiving or representing. In the *kārikā* that follow, Gauḍapāda indicates several of them.

20. *Those who know prāṇa, call prāṇa ātman-reality; those who know the bhūtas call the bhūtas reality; those who know the guṇas call the guṇas reality; those who know the tattvas call the tattvas reality.*

21. *The knowers of the fourths (pādas) call the fourths the ātman-reality and those who know the objects of senses consider sense-objects to be reality; the knowers of the lokas consider lokas to be reality; the adorers of the devas consider only the devas as reality.*

22. *Those who know the Vedas call the Vedas reality; while those who perform sacrifices call the sacrifices (yajña) reality; those who understand only the subjects of enjoyment or the object of enjoyment consider, respectively, the enjoyer or the object of enjoyment to be reality.*

23. *The knowers of the subtle sphere designate reality as subtle; the knowers of the gross sphere call reality gross; those who adore a Person, under any form whatsoever, consider that Person to be reality and those who do not believe in forms call emptiness reality.*

24. *The knowers of time call time reality; the knowers of directions call directions reality; the knowers of discussion call discussion reality and the knowers of the worlds call the worlds reality.*

25. *The knowers of manas (mind) call manas reality; the knowers of buddhi call buddhi reality; the knowers of citta call citta reality and those who know dharma and adharma call dharma and adharma reality.*

26. *Some hold that reality is comprised of twenty-five categories, others of twenty-six, others of thirty-one while others think that they are innumerable.*

27. *Those who know human relations call reality the enjoyment deriving from such relations; those who know āśramas call it āśramas; grammarians call it masculine, neuter and feminine while others know it as para (supreme) and as apara (non supreme).*

28. *The knowers of creation consider creation reality; the knowers of dissolution (laya) describe reality as dissolution and those who believe in preservation call it preservation. All these ideas are nothing but projected images (by the jīvātman).*

29. *An individual simply follows the object of knowledge presented to him. Therefore a strong aspiration towards it produces identity.*

30. *Although it (ātman) is not different from all those things, it seems however to be so. He who truly comprehends this interprets (the Vedas) correctly.*

Another mistake is that of stating that the "snake", the "garland" and therefore *prāṇa*, etc., can exist without the support of *Brahman*; that the relative, can exist without the Absolute, or dynamic movement without a static center, or a form without its subtle structure, etc. In other words, that the effect can exist without the cause.

Now the universe, for *Asparśa*, is a phenomenon-effect without a life of its own, independent of *Brahman*; or better still, becoming cannot possess life independent of Being.

31. As in dream, the magical projection of a wizard and the city of Gandharva which may be seen in the skies are considered non-real, so too this entire universe is considered non-real by those versed in Vedānta.

If the universe is phenomenon-effect, is becoming, is movement (*māyā*) that expresses itself through sounds and colors; then, seen from the Being's perspective, it is nothing but a "dream", a geometrical projection by the Great Universal

Architect, that *appears* and *disappears*, wherefore it cannot be considered as constant truth.

Compared to the absolute Constant the universe of names and forms is non-real because it is impermanent, transient, therefore it is appearance-phenomenon.

We quote some passages from western Tradition which are very significant and correspond to the *Asparśavāda* teaching. Here is how Parmenides expresses himself:

«Only one discourse about the way (μῦθος ὁδοῖο)
[remains:
That it "is". On this way there are very many
Signs: that Being is ungenerated and imperishable,
In fact it is, in its entirety, whole, immobile and without end.
Nor was it once, nor will it be, since it is now altogether
[everything,
One, continuous. In fact, what origin of it will you look for?
...What necessity ever would have compelled it
To be born?... For this reason, neither birth
Nor death Justice conceded to it...
In fact, had it been born, it would not be: nor is it, if
[it ever would have to be in the future.
So birth smolders and death is left unknown.
Nor is it divisible, because it is entirely whole and the same;
Nor is there somewhere a something more which
[could prevent it from being unity,
Nor is there a something less; but it is wholly entire,
[full of being...
For it, all of those things the mortals established,
[convinced that they were true, are just names...»[1].

---

[1] Parmenides, *On nature*, Frg. 8, Rusconi, Milan, Italy. (Italian Edition).

In Parmenides' Teaching only Being exists—which is and does not become, which is non-born (*ajāti* for Gauḍapāda) and therefore has no end, which is indivisible unity, which is neither quality nor quantity—all the rest is phenomenon-appearance which has the possibility of being only if referred to Being; in other words, there is no duality.

32. *The supreme truth is this: there is neither birth nor dissolution, nor aspirant to liberation nor liberated nor anyone in bondage.*

If things are seen from the metaphysical perspective, and only this is of interest to the *Upaniṣad* and to Gauḍapāda, one can affirm that birth and dissolution, bondage and freedom are correlative terms that can only be found at the level of the dualistic *manas*, that is they are contingent truths. Parmenides says: "δόξας δ'ἀπὸ τοῦδε βροτείας", the opinions of the mortals.

The greatest tragedy for the individual is to consider himself as contingent and perishable. It is a reductive conception of reality leading to dissatisfaction, anguish and, even, to violence.

It has been stated above that the being may follow many pathways in perfect freedom, as he may also remain "unmoving mover".

33. *This (ātman) is imagined under the guise a multiplicity of non-real objects and at the same time it is recognized as being non-dual. These multiple objects (bhāva) are imagined in non-duality itself, and as a consequence, only non-duality is favorable (constitutes bliss).*

34. *This multiple world does not exist either in an autonomous way nor depending on something else. Nor do phenomenal things exist insofar as they are different or non-different (from each other or from the Self). This is what the knowers of the Truth have declared.*

If the world is merely a phenomenon, a conformed movement (*māyā*), a becoming that appears and disappears, then it does not exist, as absolute reality, either autonomously or because it depends on other factors (such as *prāṇa, prakṛti*, etc., that are also *māyā*). In fact, as soon as its premise (*avidyā*) disappears, it vanishes like a cloud in the sky or like a dream when one awakes. Universes emerge and vanish like soap bubbles, but underlying these apparitions and disappearances there is the foundation, the Constant called *ātman-Brahman* by the *Asparśavāda*, although names are of little importance.

35. *This non-dual ātman, that is beyond all imagination and is free of phenomenal multiplicity, is fully realized by the Munis (wise ones) who have freed themselves of desire, fear, anger and are well versed in the meaning of the Vedas.*

36. *As a consequence, knowing the ātman in this manner and concentrated on non-duality, the sage behaves in the world as if he were (apparently) slow of intellect.*

37. *The Renouncer (Realized one) is above all praise and salutations; is free of ritual. The Renouncer uses the (perishable) body and the (indestructible) ātman as supports and trusts in circumstances (for the needs of the physical body).*

These last three *kārikās* are so easy for the intellect to grasp that they require no explanation, but at the same time they are so difficult to realize that for some a lifetime will not be enough.

38. *Having known truth both in the individual and universal context, the being is one and the same with Reality, which is eternal bliss.*

Comprehending through *viveka* (discernment) and resolving by means of *vairāgya* (detachment) being frees himself from the error of identifying with the individual state (the last three sheaths) and the universal one (the first two body-sheaths). In this way he realizes that sole supreme Reality, the Constant or the One-without-a-second.

Here is a summary of the fundamental points contained in the second chapter.

Commonly and in an *a priori* fashion, it is stated that the dream condition is unreal, while waking is real. Gauḍapāda demonstrates, on the contrary, that the dreaming condition is not really different from the waking state. He considers the object and the subject of perception in the two states, examines and compares them and concludes that there are no valid elements to differentiate between them in an absolute way.

Furthermore, a phenomenon, or anything else, should be seen, evaluated and judged from its own and natural operative context. No data may be measured or assessed by referring it only to the physical-dense level: this would imply that it was established *a priori,* and in absolute terms, that only one reality exists, that is the physical one, that becomes the sole point of comparison for everything else.

Thus, a dream is judged as such only upon waking, therefore, from the standpoint of the waking state; but if this conclusion is accepted then one may argue, from the dreaming position of consciousness, that waking is not real. In fact, for one who has left the physical plane to accede to *taijasa,* the former appears as a nightmare from which one is finally freed.

Having established that the two states are not dissimilar, Gauḍapāda concludes that, as they have an origin, a development and an end, they cannot be considered as absolutely real, they are, therefore, mere contingent and fleeting phenomena, or degrees of truth, but they are not *the* Reality[1]. And then: where do these contingent states come from? From the mind of the *jīva* (individual and universal) whose nature typically imagines-projects until it solidifies the image or archetype. Manifestation at different levels of condensation, is the projection of unresolved seeds of a previous *manvantara* (*Muṇḍaka Up*.: II, II, 12).

But if manifestation, or a *manvantara*, comes and goes, appears and disappears, should only annihilation and nothingness be postulated?

If the snake, or anything else, comes and goes, appears and disappears, what remains in its place?

There remains the rope, answers Gauḍapāda; there remains the Constant, *ātman-Brahman.* And it is this Constant which must be realized, rather than thought about or demonstrated. *Asparśa* is the *yoga*, that offers the certainty of our immortality and eternity.

---

[1] Reality, to be such, must be in time, in space, and outside of time and of space. A something that appears and disappears, which now *is* and then is no longer, cannot be considered Real: it can only be defined as phenomenon, appearance devoid of *aseity*.

Chapter III

Advaita Prakaraṇa

(Non-Duality)

1. *Aspirants who undergo devotional practices live under the impression of the manifest Brahman. (Yet, they think that) before creation, Brahman was not born. Therefore, such aspirants cannot but be limited in their vision.*

If Reality is one and one only, then, an individual who, through his *forma mentis*, creates dualism or divides Reality, may be considered to be under the veil of illusion. This does not prevent him, however, from seeking aid from superhuman and human Beings. In fact, a person pressed by *avidyā*, cannot but ask for help.

The question posed in the *kārikā* is notably philosophical. There are some who consider the Creator and the creature as two distinct and separate beings who will never be reunited. They consider the creature dependent on the Creator, to whom it owes devotion and to whom it accounts for its actions. They consider *Brahman*, the supreme Reality, eternally beyond time, space, cause, as having fallen into time-space-cause, in other words, they believe that the non-born has fallen into generation.

In this third chapter Gauḍapāda addresses the metaphysical problem of non-generation of *Brahman* and writes: listen to how nothing is in any way born although it appears to be born. How is it that *Brahman*, although non-born, seems to be born?

2. *Now I shall speak of That (Brahman), free of limitations, non-born and always in a state of equilibrium (identical to itself), and listen to how, nothing is in anyway born although it appears to be born.*

3. *The explanation concerning birth is this: the Self is considered as existent, in the form of individual souls, like the ether-space exists in jars; the Self, thus, exists in the form of composite things just as the ether-space exists inside jars, etc.*

4. *Just as the ether confined within jars, etc., merges fully (into boundless ether) when the jars, etc., disintegrate, so too the jīvas merge into the ātman.*

5. *Just as all the ether-space enclosed in different jars is not obscured when one of these ether-spaces, thus limited, is contaminated with dust, smoke, etc., so it happens with individuals with regard to happiness, etc.*

6. *Although forms, actions and names differ here and there, nonetheless no difference occurs within ether-space (that remains one). The same is true of jīvas.*

7. *Just as ether-space enclosed in a jar is neither a transformation nor a part of the (universal) ether, so too the jīva is neither a transformation nor a part of the supreme Self.*

8. *Just as the ignorant may think that the ether is obscured by dust, etc., so also the Self seems to be darkened to the eyes of the non-knower.*

9. *For what concerns its birth, its death, its coming and going (transmigration) or its existence in multiple bodies, ātman does not differ in anyway from ether-space.*

How is it that *ātman*, although not "fallen", seems to have fallen into bondage or into generation?

Birth implies change of state, of nature; it implies movement and duality.

Can we consider the ether contained in a jar different from the ether outside the jar?

And although the jar may undergo possible changes, in what way can the ether, which is inside, be conditioned by them?

Now one may ask: how is the jar born or, in our case, how are the various "aggregates" produced, such as the physical body, the *manas*, etc.?

«The corporeal aggregates etc., as the jars mentioned in the text, are produced by the *jīva* in a way similar to the bodies we perceive in dreams or those projected by a magician. In other words, these (bodies, etc.) are not real (from the point of view of the ultimate truth)».

Are the jar or the body (physical, of the *manas,* etc.) absolute truths opposing the absolute One?

If the reply is affirmative one is faced with several absolutes, and this is not conforming to reason.

If they are not absolute, then they must be accidents. Relativity implies that something may appear and disappear, and what appears and disappears cannot be classified as anything but as phenomenon.

An individual's psyche is capable of creating phenomena, appearances, not absolute realities.

Due to *māyā* the dreamer's ideas are "animated", they are projected upon his own screen so that they "appear" to be conscious moving actors. But these actors, or animated bodies, who have no intrinsic reality or *aseity*, cannot consider themselves either born (i.e. come into real existence), or having a specific aim in themselves. What "appears" is a graphic representation of a being which is behind appearance and disappearance.

To liken *Brahman* to the world of shadows and phenomena is not reasonable. The ether is within the jar and the jar represents the phenomenon.

Māyā is the projective capacity of being, it knows how to animate a phenomenon; it has the power to "project" and at the same time to "veil" the projected being. Or again, the being has the capacity of making itself aware of the potentials of *prakṛti*.

10. *All the aggregates (such as the body, the senses, etc.) are produced, just as in dreams, by the ātman's māyā. No valid argument could demonstrate their reality or equality or superiority.*

11. *It has been clarified, with the example of the ether-space, that the individual being, with its (five) sheaths, beginning with the gross physical one, etc., treated extensively in the Taittirīya Upaniṣad, is nothing but the supreme Self.*

A being's aggregates are not distinct from the being, they are simply its representations; but, at the same time, one cannot say that they are the being itself.

The aggregates are a particular modal impressions or dialectic moment of a being; but while these may or may not be there, the actual being is always constant. Therefore, all is *Brahman*, but not all is *Brahman*.

What the *kārikā* highlights is that these aggregates have no life of their own, they are not *aseity*, and hence there is no duality.

12. *With reference to the different dual contexts it is evident that the ether which pervades the earth is identical to that which pervades any organism; it is in this manner that Brahman is described in the Madhu brāhmaṇa (chapter of the Bṛhadāraṇyaka Upaniṣad).*

13. *The fact that the identity of the jīva with the ātman is highlighted (by the Śruti) while multiplicity is condemned, can be readily comprehended only if we accept this point of view.*

If the ether outside the jar is *Brahman*, beyond name, form, time, space and cause, then the ether confined in the jar is *ātman*. But the ether within the jar and that outside are identical, they belong to the same nature, and as the jar is not distinct from the *ātman*, in the sense mentioned above, we cannot speak of duality or of multiple Realities.

14. *The distinction between jīva and ātman, described (in the Vedic texts) before creation was spoken of (in the Upaniṣads), must be considered in a secondary sense only and refers to a future result (that is unity), because this distinction is out of place in the primary sense.*

15. *Creation has been expounded in many ways, with the help of the examples of earth, gold, sparks, etc. It is simply mentioned to generate the idea (of unity), but there is certainly no multiplicity.*

16. *There are three stages (āśramas) of life (the fourth is that of saṁnyāsin) that correspond to (the three degrees of comprehension): lower, intermediate and higher. This meditation is recommended for those (who are as yet not illuminated) merely out of compassion.*

The vedic texts, due to their particular nature, deal with duality, Unity and Non-duality, but this is done in order to respond to the various mind frames and receptive capacities of beings. There is, therefore, no contradiction; rather, there is comprehension for those who, under the sway of *avidyā*, are still unable to raise themselves up to the highest level of the teaching (*paravidyā*).

> «Two are the sciences which one must know; they who know the science of *Brahman* say that there are a higher (*para*), and a lower one (*apara*)».
>
> (*Muṇḍaka Up.*: I, 4)

A child in his insecurity needs the support of his mother and father. A youth looks after himself and sees the surrounding world as a reality which he relates to and where he participates in his own right. A mature person, once all illusions have fallen, comprehends that the world around him is a phenomenon that appears upon the great stage of life and inexorably disappears.

17. *The dualists attached to their investigations, which lead to certain conclusions, are in contradiction. But this (non-dual) vision is not in contradiction with anyone.*

Every dualism leads to disagreement and struggle.

«Just as a man's different limbs: hands, feet, etc., do not enter into conflict with one another, so is our point of view in conformity with the *Vedas*, i.e., the recognition of the unity of *ātman* in all beings does not enter into conflict with the detailed theories which, on the contrary, contradict one another».

Alienation, at all levels, is the fruit of a dualistic conception of reality.

18. *As non-duality is the ultimate truth, one may say that duality is an accident of non-duality. But the dualists maintain duality in both cases (in the absolute and in what they call relative), therefore the non dualistic position does not oppose the dualistic one.*

If all points of view are resolved in the One-without-a-second, it is true to say that the metaphysical *yoga* (*Asparśa-yoga*) does not oppose anything, while the philosophies and religions that base their belief on the duality of life are intolerant, fanatical, fideistic and absolutistic.

A metaphysical vision of life leads everything back to the sole, impersonal, indivisible, all-inclusive Principle.

19. *It is by virtue of māyā, with the exclusion of every other possibility, that this Non-born (Brahman without a second) can be differentiated. If differentiation were real, then the immortal would become mortal.*

20. *The dualists affirm the birth of what is non-born. But how can what is non-born and immortal become mortal?*

21. *The immortal cannot become mortal, nor can the mortal become immortal because there can be no change of nature.*

22. *How can a man, who believes that a being of an immortal nature can become mortal, maintain at the same time that the immortal, which is produced (manifested), can retain its immortal nature?*

The great Gauḍapāda, in these last aphorisms, reveals the most profound philosophical clarity.

These are statements that may very well be compared to those of the greatest western philosophers.

The mortal is movement and becoming, the immortal is permanent and constant.

If the universe is movement and phenomenon, will it ever be possible to equate the Constant or the immortal to it?

Desire, self-assertion, passion, etc., are becoming, movement; will it ever be possible to realize the Constant as long as they subsist?

What is there to change in a world that is already change in itself, in a world where no sooner do we define something than what is defined is forced to vanish?

What is there to be considered stable and eternal in a world whose destiny consists in birth and death?

What should a being do, constrained as one is by the chain of birth and death, other than find oneself, integrate oneself and Be?

The game of politics, of culture, of technology, etc., are a direction for those who "are not" and who hope to stop the course of the stars, not for those who have raised the veil of *avidyā*.

Immortality can never be in the mortal, just as the One-without-a-second can never be the manifold and differentiated.

23. *The Vedic texts speak explicitly of birth and māyā, but only what is maintained by the Śruti and confirmed by reason must be held to be correct, nothing else.*

«The word "birth", unless it is used in terms of projection, is devoid of all sense. Any birth whatever, whether metaphorical or effective, can refer only to an apparent possibility the cause of which is *avidyā*. The Vedic texts, in fact, declare that: "It (*ātman*) is within, without and really without birth" (*Muṇḍaka Up.*: II, II, 2)».

24. *As it is affirmed that «Here there is no multiplicity», «It is by virtue of māyā that Indra...», «The Self without being born appears multiple», it follows that It (ātman) was born through māyā.*

«If creation were real, multiplicity would have to be just as real and there should not be any texts to demonstrate their unreality. But, in actual fact there is a text which states: "Down here there is no diversity... " (*Kaṭha Up.*: II, I, 11) "He who sees multiplicity here, goes from death to death" (*Kaṭha Up.*: Ibid.)».

«Therefore, what is held by the *Vedas* and maintained by proper reasoning, such as: "He is One-without-second and free of birth and death", is the only valid meaning to the exclusion of any other whatsoever». In other words, for a possible ultimate verdict one must refer to superior Knowledge (*paravidyā*).

A multiple manifestation would imply that all existing beings should be distinct, separate and also absolute.

Now, while the absolute is completeness in itself, we are faced with the evidence of formal beings who are wanting and relative; on the other hand, if distinction or separation among the beings were absolute, how could they establish communication?

If multiplicity, or duality were absolute, ignorance and knowledge, good and evil, and all other dualities would never be resolved, and even a person's effort to struggle for his own emancipation and for a better world would be inane.

25. *With the confutation (of the adoration) of saṁbhūti, birth is denied. In the text: «Who produces it?» all cause of birth is excluded.*

«Creation is negated by the confutation of the adoration of the majestic One, as in the text "Those who adore *saṁbhūti* enter into dense darkness" (*Īśa Up.*: 12). Furthermore, if *saṁbhūti* (*Hiraṇyagarbha*) were absolutely real, such categorical disapproval would not be reasonable... This *kārikā*-verse demonstrates that there can be no cause for something whose birth takes place through the magic of ignorance. This is in keeping with the following Vedic text: "This *ātman* is not born and dies not, does not come from anywhere, does not become anything. Unborn, constant, eternal, this Ancient (Being) is not killed when the body is killed" (*Kaṭha Up.*: I, II, 18)».

26. *Given the elusive nature (of Brahman), this passage from the Śruti, «This Self who has been described as not this, not this» negates all the (dualistic) ideas that attempt to describe (Brahman). Therefore the ātman is without birth and self-unveils itself.*

Reality, if it is One-without-a-second, can never be grasped by the mind operating upon the plane of the second, therefore of duality.

«This is the *Brahman* described as not this, not this» (*Bṛhadāraṇyaka Up.*: III, IX, 26). That «demonstrates the incomprehensible nature of *ātman* and refutes the idea that it may be comprehended by the mind».

The mind may perceive and interpret only phenomena, not the noumenon; the mind, by its very nature, operates through the categories of subject and object; the mind always places all possible data in front of itself, but the Reality without a second cannot be placed in front of anyone; Reality is not the object of conceptual demonstration, *but of consciential realization.* From this perspective it is possible to comprehend how limited and naive the dianoetic philosophy in general is, with its endeavors to provide "rational" demonstration for the ultimate truth or the supreme Reality.

That such philosophy might come to positivistic agnostic conclusions was to be expected. Whoever wishes to seek Unity of life, or the Constant, by means of the sensorial mind, faces an unavoidable destiny, defeat.

Positivistic agnosticism is the outcome of mistaken premises. An incorrect dialectic approach to Reality led this current of thought to disregard and refuse the deeper and more meaningful reality of one's own being.

Once the vertical line and even metaphysics had been refuted, the only direction left to be followed was the conquest of the phenomenal, mechanical world, thus leading the individual into a completely metallic and alienated state.

27. *The birth of something that already exists may reasonably be possible only through māyā and not in the real sense. Whoever believes that things are born in the real sense, may be referring only to the birth of what is already born.*

28. *A non-reality cannot be born either as reality or as māyā; for example, the son of a barren woman cannot be born either in a real way nor through māyā.*

To affirm the birth of the existent is against reason, to affirm the birth of the non-born is absurd.

What already exists has no need to be born, and it is impossible for the non born, or the non-existent, to be born.

Śaṅkara comments: «For those who think that all is unreal, the creation of a non-existent thing is not possible either in reality or through *māyā*, because nothing of the sort is observed in the empirical experience. Similarly, neither in a real way nor through *māyā* has the son of a barren woman ever been born. Thus, the theory of non-existence of things (absolute nihilism) cannot, in truth, be maintained».

These conclusions of Gauḍapāda and Śaṅkara, the two greatest pillars of *Advaita*, are of the utmost importance, because someone might think erroneously that the *Asparśa* or the *Advaita Vedānta* propound exclusive nihilism, individualistic solipsism, or an absolute idealism that are typical of certain philosophies.

While modern culture has developed a philosophy of phenomena and becoming, refusing and disregarding Being and thus producing an incomplete philosophy, *Advaita* has developed a *realizative* metaphysics of Being, recognizing also the manifest, the phenomenon or the becoming as expressions of the manifold degrees of relative truth, as a series of systems of co-ordinates which have no *aseity*, but only *abaliety* (dependent existence), following the scholastic terminology. It is well then to carefully meditate on *Ajātivāda* and *Advaita Vedānta* to avoid falling into the errors which, alas, even some *yogis* and philosophers of India itself have fallen into, bent as they were to believe that *Advaita* has liquidated the world considering it as mere "illusion".

From the traditional *Advaita* perspective, the term "illusion" is synonymous with phenomenon, with *māyā*, with movement that creates forms, bodies or volumes to then disappear.

The universe is not, say unequivocally Gauḍapāda and Śaṅkara, like the son of a barren woman or the horns of a hare; it is not, therefore, a nothing, a non-existent. When someone sees the "snake", or manifestation, it certainly means that they perceive something. But what is it one perceives? This is the crucial point of the *Advaita* issues. Does one really perceive the supreme Truth, the Reality without second? Or does one perceive simple phenomena? And if one perceives simple phenomena will it be impossible to know the noumenon? Or may one believe that this phenomenon has no matrix and a determining and efficient cause of its own? Śaṅkara writes: «One might have the right to hold that if Reality, i.e. the Self, were eternally incomprehensible, it would be non-existent. This view could not be correct, because the effect is perceivable. Just as the effects, i.e. creation, result from the projections of a magician, who really exists, so too the perception of the effects, in the guise of the created universe, leads us to infer the existence of the *ātman*, supreme Reality, which to some extent is like a magician, substratum of the projection that we perceive as the created universe. The universal manifestation can appear only from a reality, that is, from an existing cause, like the production of effects such as an elephant, etc., caused by the mind (must necessarily come from magician-fakir who does exists).

It is not possible, however, to maintain that the *ātman* without birth (suddenly) finds itself with a real birth». Or: «Just as a truly existent entity, such as a rope for example, can turn into a snake, etc., not in reality but only through *māyā*, similarly the real and ineffable *ātman* may appear to our eyes in the form of the universe. But from the point of view of reality, the *ātman* without birth (therefore eternally existent) cannot be born in the real sense».

«How is it possible, then», Śaṅkara asks himself, «that reality be born of *māyā*?». Here is the answer:

29. *Just as in the dreaming state the mind, thanks to the movement of māyā, has the appearance of duality, similarly in the waking state the mind, through the very same movement of māyā, seems to produce duality.*

30. *There is no doubt that while dreaming, the mind, although one, appears to be dual (subject-object); similarly, in the waking state, the mind, although one, appears split.*

31. *This multiplicity, including what moves and what does not move, perceived by the mind, is always represented by the mind itself because duality is no longer perceived when the mind ceases to operate.*

32. *When the mind, as a result of the realization of truth, that is the Self, no longer thinks, it ceases to be mind and, in the absence of things to perceive, becomes non-perceiving.*

33. *Non-conceptual knowledge, which is without birth, is not different from the knowable. Brahman, eternal and non-born, is then the sole object of knowledge; thus, only the non-born knows the non-born.*

34. *It is necessary to know the behavior the mind adopts when it is pacified, that is when is free of all imagination and endowed with discernment. The condition of the mind in deep sleep is of a totally different nature and cannot be compared to the former.*

35. *The mind dozes off during deep sleep, while this does not happen when it is pacified. The mind (of the asparśin) becomes identical to Brahman, free of fear and endowed with the all-pervading light of knowledge.*

36. *Brahman is without birth, without sleep and without dreams, without name and form, eternally resplendent and omniscient. No ritual action can ever be carried out (in reference to Brahman).*

37. *Ātman is free of all verbal expression and of all mental process. It is supremely serene, eternally shining, divine absorption, unchanging and fearless.*

38. *When the mind ceases to operate there is nothing that can be accept or refused, therefore knowledge is resolved in the ātman without birth and without change.*

Just as in a dream (which, is well to remember, is not an illusion in the general sense of the word) the mind, although one and undivided, is capable of "projecting" on its own screen numberless constellations of objects causing the multiplicity of things to appear, similarly the great universal Mind (*Māhāt*) "projects" entire universes on its own immense screen that appear to our eyes now as snakes, now as garlands, trickles of water and so on.

39. *This yoga, which is called «Asparśa» (without any contact) is difficult for many yogis to comprehend, because they, who feel fear where there is none, are afraid of it.*

«This is known as *Asparśayoga*, without contact or support because it has no relation (with anything) and is therefore not in contact with anything. In any case it is described in the *Upaniṣads.*

A *yoga* of this kind is difficult to access for *yogis* lacking in true knowledge of the *Upaniṣads.* The idea is that this truth may be realized only following an impetus whose crowning is awareness of the *ātman* as the sole reality.

Yogis are afraid (of such a *yoga*), while they should not be; those without discernment fear that, by practicing this *yoga*, their individuality will be smothered, although (*Asparśa*) is beyond all fear.

Those who consider the mind and the sensorial organs like a snake superimposed upon the rope, therefore without any reality independent from *Brahman*, achieve identity with *Brahman*, without any fear, enjoying in a natural manner that eternal peace called emancipation, which does not depend on any other factor, according to our statement: "No ritual action can ever be carried out..." (III, 36). But the other *yogis* who experience the pathway (leading to Truth), who are endowed with a lower or intermediate intellect and who consider the mind separate from *ātman*, although associated with it (that is individuality separate from *ātman*), for these who do not possess the realization of the Self, who is the reality, (it is said)»:

40. *For all these (who do not follow Asparśa) lack of fear, destruction of unhappiness, awakening (of the Self) and eternal peace depend on mental discipline alone.*

Asparśayoga is the pure metaphysical *yoga* and many aspirant *yogis* are afraid of it because, still attached to their individuality or to the phenomenal snake, the instinct of self preservation predominates in them. True death occurs not when the physical body is left behind, but when the ghost of *saṁsāra* of individuality dissolves into the self-resplendent *ātman.*

Asparśayoga is the *yoga* without contact because there is no real object which the metaphysical One may relate to. It is the *yoga* which does not rest on truths made up of relations, of contacts. Every realization that culminates within the framework of relation, within the connection between subject and object is *sparśa yoga,* i.e. with relation or contact; and contact takes place between two things, two individuals. *A-sparśa yoga,* instead, is what «may be realized only following an impetus whose crowning is awareness of the *ātman* as the sole reality» and without-a-second.

41. *The mind may be dominated by an incessant effort like one which would be required to empty an ocean, drop by drop, with the help of a wisp of kuśa grass.*

42. *Whether the mind is scattered due to the objects of desire and pleasure, or whether it finds its satisfaction in sleep, nonetheless it must be brought back under control with the most suitable means, because the state of sleep is just as harmful as that of desire.*

43. *We must withdraw thought from the pleasure deriving from desire, by remembering at all times that each pleasure is accompanied by suffering. By being aware instant by instant of the non-born, what is born (that is multiplicity) will cease to be perceived.*

44. *One must awaken the mind that is in a state of deep sleep, one must lead the distracted mind back to tranquillity, we must recognize that (in the intermediate state) the mind contains within itself virtual desires. One, though, must not disturb the mind which is in harmony.*

45. *One must not enjoy happiness in that state, but, through the practice of discernment, one must reach detachment. When the mind, which dwells in a condition of stability (harmony), is urged to emerge (from such a condition) it must be brought back into itself.*

Those who consider the psycho-physical complex (individuality) as removed from its Essence, endeavor to quieten and calm the mind through discipline, thereby they foster a state of quietism.

Whoever considers individuality as the only reality resorts, in turn, to psychological and physical means. This is the road followed by certain branches of psychology and by many *gurus* who, rather than "Masters of wisdom", are good psychologists and psychotherapists.

Liberation, for these unilateral persons, consists in dominating the psyche, without ever touching that "initiatory death" which alone would allow the solution of the entire psychophysical sphere in that relative individuality.

46. *When the mind does not fall into deep sleep where it loses itself, when it is not scattered (amid objects), when it remains motionless and does not project sensorial images, then it resolves into Brahman.*

«It has been stated previously that when the mind is freed from all imagination, as consequence of the knowledge of the truth, which is *Brahman*, it grows peaceful, serene, and withdrawn, since all its supports have been removed, like a fire which has no more fuel.

It has been concluded, furthermore, that multiplicity disappears when the mind ceases to operate».

47. *This (Brahman) rests in itself, is extinction of all suffering, unutterable, supreme bliss without birth, identical to the knowable non-born, is omniscient.*

48. *No jīva was ever born, because there is no cause that may produce its birth. This is the supreme truth: nothing is ever born.*

«Of all the (relative) truths previously described as means, only this is the supreme truth: nothing is ever born in this *Brahman* or from this *Brahman*, which constitutes the ultimate reality».

Chapter IV

Alātaśānti Prakaraṇa

(On the extinction of the burning ember)

1. *I bow to that One who is the best among human beings, who through his knowledge, similar to the ether, that does not differ from the object of knowledge, has realized the dharmas (jīvas) comparable to (infinite) heaven.*

2. *I salute that yoga, taught by the very Scriptures, well known as Asparśa, free of relations, beneficial, generator of bliss for all beings, free of oppositions and contradictions.*

Śaṅkara comments: «*Asparśayoga* is the *yoga* without any *sparśa*: contact or relation with anything whatsoever; it belongs to the nature of *Brahman.* The knowers of *Brahman* call it by this name; in other terms, that *yoga* which is free of all relations is called *Asparśayoga.* It becomes bliss for all beings. Some (aspects of) *yoga*, for example austerity (*tapas*), are in any case associated with suffering, although they are said to produce intense happiness; but this *yoga* does not belong to such categories. What then is its nature? It is bliss for all beings. We can say that enjoyment of a particular kind of object may bring happiness, but not stable well-being (enjoyment, at whatever level or degree, is always dual, therefore conflictual); this *yoga*, instead, brings bliss and at the same time stable well-being because its nature is beyond impermanence. Furthermore, it is free of oppositions. Why? Because it is devoid of contradiction. To this *yoga*, taught by the Scriptures, I offer my salute».

We can say that there is only one *yoga*, but it expresses itself in different ways; and this is to provide for the different states of consciousness of the aspirants and for the particular disposition of each.

From *Haṭhayoga* to *Asparśayoga*, through *Bhaktiyoga*, *Rājayoga*, *Layayoga*, etc., there is a crescendo of positions of consciousness and of goals that are suited to the needs of different aspirants.

We have already seen that there are three states of Being plus the *Fourth*. So there are various types of *yoga*, based on psycho-physical aspects, which lead to the states of *Virāṭ*, of *Hiraṇyagarbha*, or *Īśvara*, Being par excellence. Up to this level it is possible to speak of *yoga* in the ordinary sense, that is, the joining of two data or beings that are at a distance. Thus, the *Bhakta* strives to join with his universal Beloved one and the *Rāja yogi* to reintegrate in the state of *Puruṣa* as the polar aspect of *Prakṛti*.

But when one speaks of *Asparśayoga* the term *yoga* must be taken to mean *sādhanā*, ascesis, instrument or means of solution; this *yoga* does not join, but enables one to realize Identity with what one already is. *Asparśayoga* represents the apex of all the various *yogas* that rest upon dualism and monotheism. As it is a metaphysical *yoga* (in that it attains reintegration into the *Fourth* which is, in fact, of metaphysical order) it uses as its operative tools not psycho-physical elements but *intuitive* ones. We can say that it is a *yoga* whose point of departure is based in *buddhi*.

Only the intellect, placing itself beyond time-space, knows how to penetrate the essence of *Asparśa*: intellect taken as being's superior faculty, though the majority are conditioned by intellectualism which is a degenerate form of *buddhi* and even of *manas* (imaginative empirical mind). The *jñānin* or *asparśin*, is not an intellectual or a dianoetic and empirical philosopher. Although *Asparśa* may seem the most suitable path for the intellectual, as a matter of fact it is not; as an example western intellectualism, in general terms, is discursive, critical, analytical, empirical. These are the factors which prevent one's approach to *Asparśayoga*. Swāmi Siddheśvarānanda reported that although he traveled all over Europe he never met a pure *jñāni*.

Metaphysical Knowledge, therefore *Asparśayoga,* is not in opposition with dualism and monotheism because it considers them as two points upon the circumference of knowledge; instead, the monotheistic, or the dualistic, points of view may oppose metaphysical Knowledge because they are unable to "see" the center of the circumference.

Gauḍapāda often states that *Asparśa* is the *yoga* that is not in opposition with anything, . But this is only natural because its point of view is not that of a rational philosophy nor that of a dogmatic theology, but it is set in the sphere of the Principles, where universality and synthesis of all possible points of view hold sway. Metaphysical Knowledge is the trunk which all branches of knowledge stem from, esoteric and exoteric, and it represents the immutable Pole of an entire *Manvantara*. The branches may be born and die, but this cannot happen to the trunk, which transcends time-space. One does not attain metaphysical Knowledge through works, through fideism, nor through the rationality of *manas* (although these may constitute preliminaries), but by "direct evidence", because in pure intellectuality (*buddhi*) the knower coincides with knowledge and with the object of knowledge.

Asparśa is the *yoga* without supports because the knower is left without any of the attributes of individuality, in its fullest extent; in fact when there is "direct evidence" all relational data, the ground on which individuality stands, are missing.

3. *Some seekers maintain the birth of what already exists. Others, on the contrary, maintain the birth of what does not exist.*

4. *Something that already exists cannot be reborn and something which has never existed cannot come into existence. In saying these things, these people show that they are non-dualists, therefore they affirm the absence of birth.*

5. *We approve of the theory of non-generation which, in the end, they too affirm (in their conclusions) and we do not wish to argue. Let us listen, therefore, to this (philosophy) which is free from all controversy.*

6. *The disputants (dualists) in reality maintain the birth of a positive entity that was never born. But how can a positive entity which is non-born and immortal become mortal?*

7. *The immortal cannot become mortal, nor can the mortal become immortal because not in any way can something change its own nature.*

8. *If a person believes that a positive immortal entity may come into existence, how can that person hold, then, that this immortal and immutable entity may still preserve its immortal nature?*

9. *By the word nature it must be intend that which is permanently acquired or intrinsic, inherent; that which is not produced, that which is immutable in its essential characteristic.*

In this *kārikā* we find the explanation of the concept of nature, as some believe that the intrinsic nature of something, or *aseity*, may "change" and "be transformed".

Śaṅkara comments: «The intrinsic characteristics of a thing, for example heat and light of fire, etc., do not change in time and space. Similarly what is connatural, for example the bird's ability to fly in the air, is called nature.

Whatever is not produced by some extraneous factor alien (to the thing itself), for example the tendency of water to run downwards, is also called nature. And, finally, whatever remains identical to itself must be known as such, that is as nature. The idea of the *kārikā* is this: if the nature of empirical, imagined things does not change, even more so there cannot be any change in the immortal nature of the ultimate reality, intrinsically without birth».

We were saying in the first chapter that the nature of something can neither be transformed nor be the object of discussion. Everything may be discussed except the intrinsic nature of things.

If the nature of the Real is immortal, eternal, then this can neither be born nor become mortal or contingent.

If the nature of the Infinite is infinity, It can never become finite. «The immortal cannot become mortal, nor can the mortal become immortal» (*kārikā* IV, 7).

From this standpoint it can be affirmed that the One, if it is really such, can never "be transformed" into the many nor can Being "be transformed" into becoming, nor the Absolute into relative. Then, one might ask (and starting from the proper premises) what is it that we perceive as birth, growth and death (becoming)? Here is the crucial point of the question.

Often one starts from wrong philosophical premises and, obviously, the consequences are neither logical nor reasonable.

Thus, for example, by considering becoming and the mortal as *real*, one is then unable to grasp how Being or God, call it as you will, conceived as infinite, could have fallen into the mortal and finite condition; or, again, how the imperishable and "perfect" *ātman* could have fallen into a perishable and imperfect state.

The problem set out in these terms can never be solved; it cannot because the premises, being wrongly postulated, offer no way out.

The right premises were given above, that is: considering that Being, if it is immortal, cannot suddenly become (be transformed into) mortal, nor can timelessness find itself within time, nor the uncaused in the caused, then what is the nature of those things we perceive as finite, imperfect, caused, mortal, etc.?

Considering that *Brahman-ātman* is without birth, without death, therefore beyond time-space-cause, what can all that we perceive as time-space-cause represent?

Given that the rope, in Gauḍapāda's classical example, is of the same nature of *sat-cit-ānanda*, of infinity, of timelessness, etc., that wich we see as snake, garland, the trickle of water etc. (that is, what becomes and changes), what is it?

10. *All jīvas are intrinsically free from old age and death, but, by imagining (these qualifications) and by identifying with such ideas, they are reborn through the strength of their thought, straying far from their nature.*

11. *If the cause itself is nothing but the effect it is implicitly maintained that the cause is born insofar as it is*

effect; now, how can a thing which is transformed into effect be without birth? And how can it be eternal if it is subject to disintegration?

12. *If (as you affirm) the effect is not different from the cause, then also the effect must be without birth. And if the effect is born how can your cause still be eternal, if it is identical to its effect which is subject to birth?*

13. *That disputant certainly offers no valid explanation to maintain that the effect is produced by an unborn cause. And if it is maintained that the effect is born from a cause which is also born, this will not lead to any solution either.*

14. *How can the absence of beginning, with regard to cause and effect, be asserted by those who maimtain that the effect is the origin of the cause and the cause the origin of the effect?*

15. *Those who maintain that the effect is the cause of the cause and the cause is the cause of the effect, describe evolution as if the birth of the father were to be attributed to the son.*

16. *If the cause-effect possibility exists, you must determine the order in which cause and effect follow one another because, if both appear simultaneously, there can be no causal relationship in that they would find themselves in the same situation as that of the two horns of a cow.*

17. *You are unable to establish that cause which originates from the effect. Thus, the cause that has not come into existence cannot produce a result.*

18. *If the existence of the cause depends on the effect and the existence of the effect depends on the cause, then which of the two (existential possibilities) was born first, in order to establish that the one depends on the birth of the other?*

19. *The inability to answer this question depends on your ignorance and on the impossibility of providing a sequence of succession. Thus the Sages highlight ajāti, absence of birth.*

20. *What is known as the image of the seed and of the sprout still remains to be proven. An example which offers no valid proof cannot be used to establish a hypothesis of causal relation.*

«...We have admitted that causality has a relation like the one between the seed and the sprout» maintain the dualists.

Śaṅkara comments: «The example you offer in support of the causal relation, known as that of the seed and the sprout, is on the same level as our major proposition (that is, it must be demonstrated).

Objection: Is it not a question of experience to demonstrate that the causal relationship between seed and sprout has no beginning?

Answer: This is not correct because one admits that the former has a beginning like the latter. Just as a new sprout, born from an isolated seed, has a beginning and another seed born from another sprout also has a beginning, due to the succession of birth, in the same manner the preceding sprouts, like these seeds, must have had a beginning. Thus, because every sprout and every seed within the entire chain have a beginning, it is illogical to claim eternity for any one of them. The same is true of causes and effects. If one claims that the chain of cause and effect has no beginning, we respond that this cannot be because no unity of such a series can be maintained. Those who talk of no beginning of such a succession, refuse to acknowledge the existence of a unitary entity called either a series of seeds or series of sprouts, independent of the seed and of the plant. It has, therefore, been rightly said: "How can the absence of a beginning, with regard to cause and effect, be asserted?" (*kārikā* IV, 14). Therefore, as your opinion shows absence of logic, we have not raised any verbal objection as to the conclusion. Also in ordinary experience, those who are experts in the appropriate means apt to prove the relationship between two terms (greater and lesser) of a syllogism, never use the middle term nor the indication of something yet to be established».

21. *Ignorance with regard to the preceding and the subsequent cause and effect clearly proves the absence of creation in that, if it is true that a thing is born, then why can no preceding cause for it be found?*

22. *Something, whatever it may be, is not born of itself nor of something else (nor of both contemporaneously). A thing cannot absolutely be born if it already existed, or (nothing can be born) from what did not previously exist, nor (can anything be born) contemporaneously of what already exists and what is non-existent.*

«If something already exists, then precisely because it does exist, it cannot be born a second time... If something does not exist, then due to its very non-existence it cannot come into existence, as it is proven by the example of the horns of a hare. If things were existent and non-existent at the same time they could no longer come into existence [they would annul each other] because these contradictory ideas cannot be associated with one and the same thing. Hence the statement: absolutely nothing can be born».

23. *The cause cannot be born of an effect which has no beginning; on the other hand, an effect cannot be born of a cause without origin because something which has no cause certainly has no birth.*

24. *(We must admit) that knowledge has its objects because, otherwise, duality would be annuled. And the existence of objects, maintained by other thinkers, is also admitted due to the fact that we experience pain.*

25. *In conformity with empirical reason, a cause must be attributed to a subjective impression; but from the point of view of (supreme) reality, it is maintained that external data do not constitute a cause (of perception).*

For those who find themselves under the veil of *avidyā-māyā* the external object, as separate from the subject, exists and is real. *Asparśayoga* agrees with the philosophy of objectivist realism on this score. But for *Asparśa* this objective reality is not absolute because it is the result of a *certain way* of seeing; it represents a point of view which may be taken into consideration only under certain conditions or within a certain system of co-ordinates.

From other points of view, in fact, the external object, once a part of the veil of *māyā* is lifted, appears simply as a "modification" of its substratum. For example, all the elements, like iron, nitrogen, uranium, etc., when the veil of *māyā* is removed, are nothing but electronic combinations, therefore modifications in proportion to the elementary electronic substance (today this veil has been rent). Thus, the elements seen by the "electronic consciousness" are not external to such consciousness, as the countless dream forms are not external to the form-shaping mind, though they appear external to the dreamer. On this point *Asparśa* agrees with philosophical idealism (Berkeley). But if one tears the entire veil of *māyā*, one will discover that all manifestation, or what is meant by this term (spectacle or object), is simply a chiaroscuro, continuum-discontinuum, an appearance on the screen of *That*, of *Turīya*, eternally unborn; a phenomenon not real in itself, just as nightly dreams, chemical elements and everything in the universe cannot be real-absolute.

Then, the mind itself is nothing but a chiaroscuro which appears and disappears, because it was never born as independent reality (with this, *Asparśa* goes beyond subjective idealism). We may note that *Asparśayoga* contemplates three degrees of truth-knowledge: one resulting from *avidyā* (sensorial knowledge), one resulting from *vidyā* (suprasensorial knowledge) and one resulting from *Turīya* (knowledge by identity).

26. *Mind does not enter into relationship with (external) objects, nor does it enter into relationship with the ideal appearances of objects, because, according to the reasons given, an object has no real existence and the idea-appearances are not disjoined from the mind.*

«Since there is no external object, the mind does not enter into contact with an object, nor does it enter into contact with ideas that appear as objects because they are a modification of the mind; this is evident in dreams because, according to the preceding argument (chap. II), an object is as unreal in the waking state as it is in the dream state. Nor is ideation, which appears in the guise of an object, different from the mind; after all, it is always the mind, like in a dream, which appears as object, for example, as a jar, etc.».

In dreams there are neither objects nor ideas which are separate from the dreamer's mind, even if to that person they "appear " to be separate (subject-object duality). Thus, in the universe of waking there are neither objects nor ideas separate from the "universal Dreamer".

The subject and object of every dimension and degree are polar opposite data which have no nature of reality because they are projections of a substratum common to both.

27. *The mind in none of the three temporal stages (past, present, future) enters into contact with external objects. (On the other hand) as there are no external objects, how can there be a false perception of them without any causal relationship?*

«*Objection*: If the mind appears like a jar, even though unreal, then there must be erroneous knowledge. And if this is the conclusion, you must in some way indicate which one is the correct knowledge capable of explaining this error.

Here is the answer: In the three stages (past, present, future) the mind never relates with any cause, that is, with external objects. If it were to enter into a relationship with an object at any given moment, such a relationship would give the idea of exact knowledge from the point of view of reality, and compared with such knowledge, the conception of the jar, etc., might be considered erroneous knowledge. But the mind never has any relationship with external objects. Therefore, how can there be, for that mind, erroneous knowledge, if there is no object as a cause?

In other words, there is no false knowledge because it is in the nature of mind itself to take on modifications like, for example, the jar, etc., although this is not of absolute reality.

The text which begins with: «In conformity with empirical reason, a cause must be attributed...» (*kārikā* IV, 25), and which represents the point of view of the subjective idealists, is approved by the Master (Gauḍapāda) because it confutes the vision of those who believe in external objects. However, now he himself uses the same argument (that of the idealists) as middle term to demolish their own point of view».

Opposers seek to render "positive" and real ignorance (*avidyā*) which is the cause of erroneous knowledge (empirical).

In order to be positive and real, knowledge-ignorance should have an equally real, positive and self-existent object. After all, the subject, the object and knowledge-ignorance are not absolute realities, therefore both knowledge and ignorance, in the ordinary sense, belong to the sphere of *avidyā*.

Avidyā is not ignorance of something external, nor non-knowledge about the description of event-objects, but is ignorance on the nature of Being. Thus, this type of *avidyā* has no terms of comparison, is not an empirical relational datum because, we can say, it is ignorance of *metaphysical* order. To seek the cause of *avidyā* means to fall again into the illusion of causality, it is the snake biting its own tail.

28. *The mind, therefore, has no birth, nor the things it perceives have birth. Those who perceive the birth of their mind are similar to those who see birds' footprints impressed on the air.*

Kārikās from 25 to 27 express the vision of subjective idealists and Gauḍapāda agrees with their conclusions, but not in absolute terms. In fact, in the above *kārikā* he outlines his real point of view which goes beyond subjective idealism. Neither does Gauḍapāda agree with the absolutist nihilism of other philosophical schools, which state that all is emptiness, even the perceiving subject. If all is emptiness there must be a perceiving subject who affirms this emptiness, therefore the subject cannot be emptiness, otherwise we would reach this absurdity: emptiness affirms emptiness, nothingness affirms nothingness.

Thus it is possible to comprehend how *Asparśavāda* is neither nihilist nor objective-realist (according to which only the external object is real), nor idealist, although of the latter two schools of thought it shares in some of the aspects at certain levels. It is essentially of the metaphysical order.

29. *What is non-born (according to the disputants) takes birth. As the absence of birth represents its very nature, one can conclude that, in no way, can a thing change its nature.*

30. *Moreover, if (as some claim) the world were without beginning it would have to be imperishable. Thus, there could not be liberation which has a beginning.*

31. *That which is non-existent in the beginning and in the end, must, necessarily, be (non-existent) in the intermediate stage. Although objects are non-real, they are, nonetheless, perceived as real.*

32. *Their usefulness (in the waking experience) is contradicted by dream. Therefore, due to the fact that (objects) have a beginning and an end they are rightly considered as non-real.*

33. *All data are non-real in dreams because they are seen as being inside the body; how can all such data exist within this narrow space?*

34. *It is not possible to maintain that a sleeper exits (from the body) to experience objects, due to the time-space incompatibility for such a journey. Furthermore, nobody in the waking state continues (to be) in the place of the dream.*

35. *A discussion with friends and others (in dreams) has no confirmation in the waking state, and anything acquired in a dream state is no longer possessed upon waking.*

36. *Furthermore, in dreams the body is non-real because there is another body seen by others. As in the case of the body (in dreams) so also a thing perceived by the mind is devoid of reality.*

37. *Since a dream is experienced in the same way as the waking state, it is held that the former is the outcome of the latter. In actual fact, though, the waking state is considered such only by the dreamer because it is the cause of his particular dream.*

38. *Because birth is not a proven fact, the Śruti affirms that everything is without birth. Besides, the unreal cannot be born of the real.*

39. *Struck emotionally by the apparent reality of objects in the waking state, an individual sees these same things in dreams. And having seen non-real objects in dreams one does not see them again in the waking state.*

«*Jagarite*: in the waking state an individual *dṛṣṭvā*: sees an object *asat*: non-real, like the snake imagined instead of the rope and, becoming emotionally *tanmayaḥ*: upset, he then sees (that object) *svapne*: also in dreams, thereby imagining the same subject-object duality as in the waking state. In addition, unless one resorts to imagination, *asat*: the unreality seen *svapne*: in dreams *na paśyati*: is not seen in the waking state. The word *ca*, in the text, indicates that the causal relationship is not regularly observed between the state of waking and that of dreaming. Thus, some things which we see in the waking state, at times, are not known to us in the dream state. As a result, it is not from the point of view of the ultimate truth that one may declare that the waking condition is the cause of dreams».

40. *The unreal cannot have the unreal as its cause, nor can the real be born of the real, nor again can the real be born of the unreal, nor, finally, can the unreal be born of the real.*

«*Na asti asat*: there can be no unreal datum which *asaddhetukam*: has another unreal thing as its cause: thus a city in the air, for example, cannot have as its cause another unreal thing, as for example the horns of a hare; *na asti sat*: nor can there be a real thing, a jar, which is produced by an unreal datum, like the horns of a hare. In the same way there cannot be a real datum, for example a vase, that is the product of another real (already existing) datum, for example a jar. How can we conceive a non-reality produced by a reality? Furthermore, there is no possible or imaginable kind of causal relationship (besides these cases). As a consequence, discerning people come to the conclusion that it is impossible to demonstrate any kind of causal relationship whatsoever.

Again, to remove all traces of causal relation between the waking and the dream states, it is maintained that»:

41. *As someone in the waking state, due to lack of discernment, may come into contact with illusory objects*

believing they are real, so too in dreams, due to erroneous knowledge, one may see (real) objects which are of the nature of dreams.

«*Yathā viparyāsāt*: like someone, due to lack of proper knowledge, *jāgrat*: in the waking state may imagine *acintyān*: unthinkable things, like the snake, etc., projected on the rope, *bhūtavat*: and consider them real, so too in dreams, *viparyāsāt*: due to lack of proper discernment, imagines or visualizes objects, such as elephants, etc., which belong only to the state of dreams, taking them for real».

42. *The causal process of creation has been described by the Sages out of love for those who, constrained by experience and behavior (inherent in their state), are wont to claim the existence of the real universe, terrified by the absolute non-manifestation of the being.*

«For those who *upalambhāt*: experience and follow *samācārāt*: behavior adequate to the duties of social class and stages of life and believe in the reality of the objects experienced, out of love for them, who are fundamentally serious in their efforts, faithful, but endowed with a limited mind, the non-dualistic Sages have spoken of *jātiḥ*, creation.

The theory of creation, however, has been described with the idea that it may be accepted by them only provisionally, because gradually, by practicing *Vedānta*, knowledge of the unborn and non-dual Self unveils to them spontaneously. But (with reference to creation) the Sages have not spoken from the point of view of the ultimate truth. And this is right, because these non-discerning people (to whom this limited teaching is addressed) are faithful in their vedic practices, but, because of their not too sharp intellect, they are always terrified by the real without birth: that is, they fear that this may lead to their annihilation».

Human experience is characterized by the sense of ego (*ahaṁkāra*) and by the projecting and imaginative *manas*. And the *ahaṁkāra* has grown so rooted in human consciousness that it is extremely arduous to overcome it.

To realize an impartial, equanimous consciousness, in which the sense of ego begins to vanish, is already difficult, but it is even more difficult to resolve into "universal consciousness" whith which all reference to you and I, to mine and yours is gone by. Just as at the individual level one is aware of one's own formal or corporeal totality and nobody perceives a hand separately from an arm or the eyes from the face, etc., so, at the universal level, the various modalities and states of the Being are not felt as separate.

But one point should be clarified: for the traditional East, consciousness is a reality that subsists even without objects, it is therefore *aseity*, while for the non-traditional western consciousness is always a "function" of the psycho-physical individual, that vanishes when the individual dies.

For *Vedānta*, Being is *sat-cit-ānanda*, that is, Being aware of itself as completeness-fullness, since it is *ānanda*: bliss-fullness-completeness. Now, when the individual transcends *ahaṁkāra*, which is a product of *avidyā* that causes an apparent separation between being and Being, its underlying essence (or its incarnate reflection, or its manifest ray of *ātman*) is not annihilated, nor annulled in an amorphous and unconscious state (in the universe nothing is unconscious) rather it rejoins its true source that is Being, and Being includes not only "human consciousness" but is the totality of universal Consciousness.

When one considers the problem of the death of individuality (we are speaking here of the death of the individuality, not of the physical body), many are the reasons that create and lead to non-rational reactions: fear of the unknown, a sentimental attitude towards the human condition, fear of annihilation, mistakenly considering consciousness as a simple attribute of the psycho-physical complex, religious conceptions that place creature-Creator duality in absolute terms, addressing the problem without the right approach. Some find it hard to think of themselves as Being, but this is because they "feel" themselves to be, above all, limited individuality or because, if they try to conceive of themselves as Being, their individuality, for obvious reasons, responds in a negative way. But a being is not just "individuality"; this one is a mere appendix, an extension, a modality; we will say that it is just an accident of the total possibilities of a being, whose nature coincides with Being.

Another wrong approach is that of believing that by losing its individuality being dissolves into "matter" without consciousness, thus confusing Being and being with primordial substance, with *materia prima*; this one instead represents the pole which is complementary (and not opposed) to *essence*, while Being and being are beyond essence-substance, the two poles from which formal manifestation proceeds. In *Vedānta* terms the universal substance is *prakṛti*, Plato's χώρα, and being does not dissolve in it; what dissolves in *prakṛti* are its body-vehicles.

The manifest *beings* are sparks of the primordial Fire, and their nature is identical with such Fire.

The cult of human individuality, separated from the Source, reaches such a level of egotism and exclusiveness as to consider the human expression as the only important form of existence, the one to which the entire intelligent universal life has devoted its attention.

There are many spiritual doctrines which are anthropocentric, although they admit of a soul with characteristics that are not specifically or exclusively human; others go as far as being individuocentric, if we are allowed the term, because they postulate the "individual divine" as the absolute reality thus conceiving Being as a mere individuality.

An individuality has a character which distinguishes it from other individualities, it has its own note or complex of exclusive notes peculiar to that "particular" individuality; when it comes to it, individuality is a factor of *distinction*, of differentiation, of separation, of indication vis-à-vis other individualities or other possible data. Atomism and pluralism, but not monism, admit absolute individuality.

To attribute this type of individuality to Being or to the very essence of the human being means introducing distinction, separation and comparison into Being; but whom may Being be separated or split from? Whom may Being be compared and assimilated to?

In the eastern and western Traditions use has always been made of two terms (although often reversed) to indicate the human psycho-physical complex and the universal Being. The two terms are individuality for the former and Personality for the latter. Totality, nature and synthesis characterize the term person; it refers to male and female, and in the juridical context it is attributed to general rather than specific factors; to move into the particular or the individual plane some other term must be added such as *physical* person, *psychic* personality, *juridical* person, etc. In the Christian theological context one speaks of three divine Persons (Trinity), not of three individualities which would have no sense; nor of two different natures in a Person. Again, one speaks of God-person and not of God-individual.

«The term person originally indicated the mask with which ancient Greek theater represented a certain character. When the use of masks declined, the word indicated the character itself, and then it went on to indicate the *human being*, who is not merely *individual*, that is an organic joining of assembled parts, but a conscious and intelligent being, a fundamental unit of thought, feeling and action»[1].

Human individuality therefore should not fear for its own death because if it discovers its own Essence it will come to realize that death is nothing but the birth of the Person-Being; but how many are capable of abandoning anthropomorphism, anthropocentrism and individuocentrism?

«Although they should not be *yogis*» comments Śaṅkara «are afraid (of *Asparśayoga*); the non-discerning ones fear that, by practicing this *yoga*, their individuality will be extinguished, although (*Asparśa*) is beyond all fear».

43. *Those who are terrified of the non-born, based on their experience of duality, deviate from the right pathway, but the errors that stem from accepting creation do not bear fruit because the error is insignificant.*

The *ātmā* consciousness is not beyond Being, outside Being, under or over Being, it never "came out" (was born) of Being so that on the one hand we would have Being and on the other being, individuality or the universe; being is within Being, moves within Being, dwells within Being. Consciousness has simply shifted its perspective; being-consciousness,

---

[1] C. Ranzoli, *Dizionario di scienze filosofiche*, Hoepli. Milano. Italy. (Italian Edition).

circumscribing itself by means of *upādhi*-bodies, has directed its focus on these, deluding itself into believing itself to be individuality.

In more specific terms one may say that individuality is born as effect of *ahaṁkāra*. This one is simply a prism which refracts and particularizes the unity of pure *ātmā* consciousness.

Duality is the effect of a shift in identity, in consciousness. The air contained in a jar has created identity with the jar rather than with the infinite air outside of it.

The "fall" represents an error of perspective, but it is not absolute, because the air contained in the jar can never be separated from nor can it differ from that outside the jar. And the "fall" endures until this *perspective* (*avidyā*) is solved, or consciousness turns towards Totality.

What is in store for those who believe that they have "come out" of Being?

They deviate from the right path, but the errors which emerge from accepting creation and duality do not bear *real* fruits because only by delusion can they believe they come out of Being. In other words, they are sleeping gods who, sooner or later, will have to awaken.

44. *Just as an elephant, born of the art of a magician, is considered real because it is perceived and because its behavior is in line (with that of an elephant), thus it is claimed that a perceived datum is real.*

45. *It is consciousness, without birth or motion, not gross and at the same time tranquil and non-dual, that seems to be born, move and possess qualities.*

46. *Thus consciousness-mind is non-born and souls are, likewise, without birth. Those who know that do not fall into error-pain.*

47. *Just as the movement of a burning ember seems to posses straight lines or curves, so consciousness in movement appears to be the knower and the known.*

48. *Just as a burning ember when it is not in motion is free from appearance and from birth, so too consciousness when it is not in motion remains free from appearance and birth.*

49. *When the burning ember is in motion, appearances (erroneously perceived) do not come to it from anywhere. Nor do they go anywhere when the burning ember is motionless, nor do they return to it.*

50. *Appearances do not come from the burning ember because of their lack of substantiality. In the case of consciousness too, the same occurs because the appearances are always identical.*

If one rotates a burning ember, the geometrical forms obtained are not real-substantial, but appearances; they are *phenomena* which appear and disappear, they come from nowhere nor do they return to the ember when it stops. From this stems the insubstantiality of *māyā* as apparent geometrical movement; it comes from nowhere and returns to nowhere. At the touch of Realization, ignorance vanishes like mist in the wind; looking for ignorance is like looking for the footprints of birds in the air, or the objects in our dreams once we awaken.

51. *When consciousness is in motion (as in dreaming and waking) the appearances (perceived) do not come to it from anywhere. Nor do they go somwhere else when consciousness is at rest (in deep sleep), nor do they enter into it.*

52. *Neither do they exist within consciousness itself because they lack substantiality, they are beyond comprehension because they are without any cause-effect relationship.*

53. *A substance may be the cause of another substance and a datum may be the cause of another datum different from itself. But souls (jīvas) may not be considered either as substance or as something different from something else.*

54. *Thus external beings are not produced by consciousness, nor is consciousness the product of external beings. Therefore the Sages confirm the absence of cause and effect.*

55. *Cause and effect emerge when there is mental representation of causality. When this representation ceases so too does causality.*

56. *As long as there is mental representation of causality, the endless wheel of births and deaths continues to turn. But when the thought of causality is resolved, births and deaths cease to come about.*

57. *Everything is born due to empirical illusory vision, therefore there is nothing which is permanent. From the point of view of reality, everything is (ātman) without birth, hence a condition called annihilation cannot exist.*

Birth, considered as the coming out of Being, does not exist; it is only by veiling or by shifting perspective that it is possible to speak of birth. But, from the point of view of the supreme Reality there is neither birth nor death, therefore there is no annihilation.

58. *The beings that are born, in reality are not born because their birth is seen through māyā and māyā itself has no absolute reality.*

59. *From an illusory (phenomenal) seed an equally illusory sprout is born; it is neither eternal nor destructible. The same is true of all beings.*

60. *If one consider all beings without birth, it follows that there is no place for the notions of eternal and non-eternal. No absolute affirmation may be made for beings for which not even adequate verbal expressions may be found.*

All relational terms have no reality whatever within the sphere of *Brahman* without-a-second: even the terms finite and infinite, relative and absolute, cause and effect, etc., have no value upon the plane of the ultimate Truth. If we have spoken of Absolute, of Knowledge, of Infinite with reference to *Brahman* this is simply for the sake of communication.

Brahman is beyond all possible polarity, duality and relational terms because it is, in fact, *Asparśa*, that is without relation with the world of relational duality.

Also the *Śruti* (*Taittirīya Up.*: II, IV, 1) states: «From which words recede...».

61. *Just as in a dream the mind modifies itself producing the appearance of duality, similarly in the waking state the mind modifies itself producing dual notions.*

62. *There is no doubt that in dreams the mind, although one, appears in the guise of dual aspects, so too the waking state, although one, seems to be characterized by duality.*

63. *The jīvas, born of an egg, from fermentation, etc., which the dream experiencer sees as existent in all ten directions (of space) as he wanders in the world of dreams, are mere objects of his mental perception.*

64. *(Those forms) do not exist independently from its mind; in the same way it is admitted that the mind of one who dreams is not the object of perception except for the dreamer.*

65. *The beings, whether born of an egg or due to fermentation, that the experiencer of the waking state sees as existent in all ten directions (of space) as he wanders in the sphere of the waking state, are simply objects of perception.*

66. *(Such objects) do not exist independently of its mind. Thus the mind in the waking state is nothing but an object of perception for one who is awake.*

67. *Both (mind and being) mutually perceive each other. If one asks whether one exists independently of the other, the answer is no; both are equally indiscernible separately because one cannot be known except by the other.*

The mind and the projected object-beings are modifications of the mind itself. In other words even the subject-object polarity is a comparative term which has no reality from the point of view of *Brahman*.

68. *Just as a being seen in dreams is subject to birth and death, so too all these entities appear and disappear.*

69. *Just as a being evoked by the imagination of a magician is subject to birth and death, so too all these beings appear and disappear.*

70. *Just as a being created by any artifice whatsoever is subject to birth and death, so all these beings appear and disappear.*

71. *Absolutely no being whatever was ever born because no cause ever was for such birth. The ultimate truth is that absolutely nothing is born.*

All individual formal beings are born and die, appear and disappear, like the formal geometry of that burning ember that was mentioned before.

In these *kārikās* the term "being" is equal to formal individuality or to subject in relation to its object. The *jīva* (living soul) is itself a subject related to an object, represented by the various *upādhis*-bodies; it and the *upādhi* both appear and disappear and only *Brahman-ātman* remains.

72. *This duality, characterized by subject-object, is a simple mental modification. But (from the point of view of the supreme reality) the mind does not enter into contact with any independent external object, therefore it is without relation (Asparśa).*

73. *That which from the empirical point of view appears as imaginary has no (real) existence from the point of view of absolute reality. Thus, whatever is held from the empirical point of view by other schools of thought has no absolute reality.*

74. *Just as (the dualists) maintain that, from the empirical point of view the soul is subjected to birth, so (the non-dualists), again from this point of view, hold that the soul is without birth; however, viewed from the ultimate truth, we cannot even speak of without birth.*

One can notice that Gauḍapāda takes great care to make the true metaphysical perspective comprehensible. Birth and non-birth, movement and immobility, mortal and immortal, real and unreal, etc., as already mentioned, are always relational, therefore empirical, truths.

75. *There is an evident, intense desire for false objects, but multiplicity does not exist. By realizing the non-existence of multiplicity one becomes free of intense desire for non-real things, so that one is not subject to birth.*

For the *asparśin* every object of desire declines, not because it is inhibited, but because he consciously recognizes that every datum is simply appearance and disappearance. The majority of individuals, alas, thirsts for and are constrained by indefinite appetites, and the history of humanity is one of conquest, accumulation, avidity and violence at all levels. When you deprive certain individuals of their objective acquisitive *supports* they may collapse and go adrift upon the plane of uncertainty and bewilderment. Others, rather than see their fleeting conquests and their "ideals" vanish, are capable of conceiving a philosophy based on compensations, they are prepared to invent truth.

One may say that most human beings, in search of desires, have obliged and oblige others to follow the philosophy of sensorial gratification of *māyā* and have constructed and go on constructing the portentous "object forging machine" in order to offer the non-illuminated weak a momentary illusion.

The *asparśin*, does not, after all, *renounce* the things of the world because, from the point of view of the ultimate truth, and only that matters to the *asparśin,* these things... are not. The position of consciousness of the *saṁnyāsin-asparśin* is not renunciation in the ordinary sense because this term presupposes something that must be renounced. We may also say that it is the attitude of the dualists that imply true renunciation, abandonment, detachment from the things of the world and from the world because they believe objective data to be real; but for the *asparśin* there is no renunciation, flight or detachment to be carried out: the world, with its various vital expressions is simply the snake superimposed upon the rope, and when one realizes *Brahman* there are no longer things to detach from, they have disappeared.

76. *When the mind does not perceive the higher, intermediate and lower causes, it is freed from birth. Because, how could there be effect without any cause?*

«The loftiest (higher) causes are those duties prescribed for the social orders and for the stages of life, carried out by those who are not attached to the results. They lead to the state of consciousness of the Gods, and others; they are purely virtuous acts. The intermediate causes consist of those duties associated with certain practices not connected to religion whose observance permit a being to rise to the human state, etc. The lower causes are those particular tendencies known as totally irreligious and which lead to birth among subhuman beings, etc. But when the mind resolves into *ātman*, which is One-without-a-second and free of all imagination, it no longer perceives causes, higher, intermediate and lower, exactly because they are imagined through ignorance (*avidyā*), in the same way as certain phenomena seen in the sky by children are not perceived by a discerning adult. Now the mind (*jīva*) no longer undergoes birth in the form of Gods or other ones, forms which constitute the effects of the higher, intermediate and lower orders. When there is no cause there is no effect either, just as without a seed a flower cannot be born».

77. *The absence of birth attained by consciousness when it is free of cause is constant and absolute; this birthless state pre-existed its liberation.*

78. *Having realized the absence of causality as the ultimate truth, one attains to the state of liberation which is free from pain, desire and fear.*

79. *It is because of its attachment to the non-real objects that the mental (jīva) pursues such objects, but returns to its intrinsic nature when it ceases to be attached to them (recognizing their absolute non-reality).*

80. *When consciousness has detached itself (from objects) and no longer enters into activity, it achieves the state of quiet. Thus the Sage, realizing such quiet, reaches true harmony which is without birth and non-dual.*

81. *This (Reality) is without birth, without sleep, without dreams and self-resplendent because ātman is always resplendent by its very nature.*

Brahman, or the *Fourth*, is beyond the three states mentioned, which correspond by analogy to the states of waking, dreaming and dreamless sleep.

82. *Due to the desire for any object whatsoever, the Lord (ātman) is easily hidden, so that it is difficult to discover.*

Due to identification with the *upādhis* and with the three *guṇas*, one loses the identity between the self and *Turīya*. This is the condition of Narcissus who adheres to his own image to the point of losing his identity.

83. *Asserting that the Self «exists», «does not exist», «exists and does not exist» or again «does not exist in the absolute sense» the non-discerning being certainly veils it with ideas of change, of unchangeability, of mutability and immutability, and of non-absolute existence.*

«Some disputants accept the idea that the Self exists. Others, that is those who believe in the fleetingness of things, hold that it does not exist. And the absolute nihilists say, "it does not exist", "it does not exist". Those who hold that the *ātman* exists, consider it changeable, but different from the impermanent things like the jar. Those who claim that the *ātman* is non-existent base themselves on a constantly changing nature. Those who declare that *ātman* is existent and non-existent, consider it of both types because it refers to both the changeable and the unchangeable. The last ones claim that the Self is absolutely non-existent. Thus the four categories examined claim: one existence, another non-existence, another still contemporaneous existence and non-existence and yet another the absolute non-existence (of *ātman*). But these theories stem from prejudice such as changeability, immobility, the concurrence of existence and non-existence and absolute negation. Thus these people are not discerning and with their theories they undoubtedly veil the Lord (the Self)».

84. *These ones (presented) are the four alternative theories and, due to our attachment to one of them, the Lord (ātman) remains hidden from vision. One who sees the Lord as untouched by these (superimpositions) is omniscient.*

85. *What further effort could be made after reaching omniscience in all its fullness and the non-dual state of the brāhmaṇa, a state without beginning, evolution or end?*

Ritual or social action, the outcome of desire, has its validity until one finds the true object of ritual and desire. The "accomplished ones", those who have found themselves again, what further actions could they perform?

As long as one is not, action is a necessity, but when one is, all kind of enchaining action-activity comes to an end. Every type of action is something non-complete. Being comes from nowhere and goes nowhere. There is nothing to "reach" because Being is. Action which "tends to" is an illusion that defers one from being aware of the Self.

«The idea is that any action (or desire) whatsoever becomes useless, as also the *Gītā* (III, 18) states: "Neither action nor non-action may ever be of interest for such a being in this world, he no longer depends on anything nor, for any purpose may he find refuge in beings"».

86. *The realization (of Brahman without birth) confers upon brāhmaṇas a natural and spontaneous quiet. Having known this, the illuminated person dwells (definitively) in peace.*

87. *The common state (of waking) is that of duality, which consists in things belonging to the empirical reality suitable to be experienced. The ordinary state (of dreaming) is that in which one admits dual experience although the objects are not real.*

88. *Tradition holds that there is another state without content and without experience. So are proclaimed by the Sages also the knowable, knowledge and the known object.*

«That which is non-substantial and free of experience or, in other words, what is without subject and object, is maintained by Tradition to be beyond the usual empirical experience. It is, therefore, suprasensible because while normal experience consists in subject and object, in this state instead there is absence of this duality; it constitutes the seed of every possibility and is called the state of deep sleep».

89. *When the objective triplicity is known in succession and when the supreme Reality becomes self-revealed, then, for beings of high intellect, the state of omniscience is eternally unveiled.*

«Because the common-gross, the subtle states, etc., are presented as objects to be known in succession, some might draw the conclusion that they have real existence. So it is said»:

90. *The things to avoid, those to know, those to accept and those to render ineffective must be comprehended from the beginning. The three conditions, apart from that of realization, are considered traditionally as fantasy produced by ignorance.*

«The three states, beginning with the common one (of waking) must be rejected. That is, just as we have to reject the illusory snake superimposed upon the rope, similarly we must not take into consideration waking, dreaming and deep sleep because these are not the Self. What must be known (realized) in this context is the supreme reality free from those four theories (of the sophists). The things that must be accepted by a disciple, having renounced threefold desire (those concerning progeny, attachment to earthly goods and to heavenly ones), are the disciplines called: wisdom and the fruit that stems from knowledge and from meditation. Finally, the things which must be rendered ineffective: impurities like attraction, repulsion, deception, etc., are also known as passions. All these things, that is those which must be avoided, accepted, made ineffective and realized, must be thoroughly known by the disciple from the beginning. But they, apart from what has to be realized, that is, *Brahman*, the sole reality, are perceived because of our imagination».

91. *All dharmāḥ must be known as belonging to the nature of ākāśa and as eternal. They must not, therefore, ever be considered as in the least multiples in any place.*

92. *All souls are, for their own nature, resplendent from their origin and eternally immutable. One who has realized this vision has freed himself from the need of further knowledge and has unveiled immortality.*

93. *Souls are, from their very origin, tranquil, non-born and, by their very nature, totally detached and non-different, just as reality itself is without birth, uniform and pure.*

All *dharmas*, *puruṣas* or *jīvātmans*, as reflections of *ātman*, must be known as non-formal, eternal, non-born and pure. The Reality which permeates the world of phenomenon-spectacle, is one, homogeneous, balanced, without birth and without end, and we, at some levels, are this Reality without-a-second.

94. *There can be no perfection for those who have ideas of multiplicity, who walk along the pathway of duality and who speak of plurality. Therefore, traditionally, they are considered worthy of compassion.*

95. *Insuperable knowledge will belong only to those who are firm in their conviction regarding that which is without birth and constant. But the common person cannot grasp this reality.*

96. *It is held (by Tradition) that the very knowledge, inherent in birthless souls, is non-born and free of relations. As this knowledge is not related to any object it is said to be unconditioned.*

97. *If the non-discerning person holds even the slightest notion of birth, etc., there is always attachment; it is useless, then, to speak of destroying the veiling screen.*

The knowledge mentioned here is metaphysical knowledge, inherent in Being itself; it is knowledge by identity, therefore not the imaginative knowledge of *manas* which is born and dies.

The *sādhanā* of *Asparśayoga* consists, therefore, in considering gross (*Virāṭ*), subtle (*Hiraṇyagarbha*) and germinal or noumenal (*Īśvara*) objects as belonging to the domain of relations, duality, rapport and contact; this implies, from the metaphysical perspective, that these concern the sphere of non-reality.

Reality, as such, must be non-dual, free of relation, free of rapport; in other words, it must be *Asparśa.*

The Infinite has neither size (big or small) nor duration (succession of moments, long or short); the Infinite is beyond all size and duration because it is neither space nor time, even though these may be extended to the unlimited.

98. *No soul is under any veil; all dharmas are, by their own nature, pure, illuminated and free from eternity. Thus (endowed by nature as they are, with the power of knowledge) it is said that they know.*

99. *The knowledge of the illuminated being, which is all-pervading, has no relation with any object; so, souls have no relation to objects. This point of view was not expressed by the Buddha.*

So, the *dharmas* have no relationship with objects, they are *Asparśa*; this implies that they are of the nature of *Brahman Nirguṇa*, of *Turīya*, without birth and without end. But some are only able to comprehend the Creator-creature duality, they are able to conceive only the theological dimension. Others, incapable of grasping the "immobile Mover", are forced to outline an infinite evolution of the *dharma*, without ever reaching perfection. To hold that a God creates the various *dharmas* and universes and then does not grant them the capability of ever being reintegrated in It, means admitting a series of incongruities and gaps from which it is almost impossible to emerge, besides the fact that a God thus conceived shows a good deal of cynicism.

It can be stated that:

1. If God is cause and beings effects, one must admit that the effects can be reintegrated into the cause, because they are merely its modifications. So, within the gross dimension, energy resolves into mass and mass can resolve into energy. An effect cannot be distinct from its cause, nor can, therefore, cause and effect be considered as absolute duality. On the contrary, the effect is the very cause which configures itself as a specific "modality" of being (cp. chap. IV, 11 ff.).

2. If self-aware beings are emanations or creations of God's, then they are of the same nature as God himself, even though they express "parti\cular" aspects of his, since nothing may come into existence from nothingness or from an absolute non-reality. If nature is identical, one may ask how a *sole* nature may find itself in opposition to itself.

3. If self-aware beings had no possibility of "comprehending" their "Parent" and to return to Him, they would be eternally lacking, incomplete, alienated and orphans, and, if this were the case, for them there could be no expansion of consciousness, nor perfection capable of filling their *eternal* and *absolute* incompleteness.

From this perspective the conception of evolution postulated by the dualists is but a superfluous "concession" because it does not solve the essential problem, and it would be nothing but a game of mockery.

4. If beings and the universe are creations with a beginning, they must also have an end; now, when they end where will they go? Will they dissolve into nothingness? Nothingness does not exist in reality, it can exist only as a mental category.

If, instead, they have no birth nor end, then they are as infinite and eternal as the uncaused cause, and as two parallel or opposed infinites cannot coexist because they would annul each other, one can deduce that the two cannot but be undivided unity.

5. If God is Person and has in itself Intelligence and Power, why should it chose to *create* or emanate some beings or things which in turn would be eternally lacking and alienated?

And even if one were to postulate a mediator between God and human beings, acting as a link, nonetheless the fact would remain that human beings would be deprived just the same of "rejoining" the "Parent".

6. If God, in that totality, is absolute oneness, can a non-reducible duality ever be found in it?

From the brief illustration above, one may deduce that the *dharmas*, in their deepest essence are nothing but the non-engendered cause, and they cannot but be so, and is only *apparently* that they can believe themselves to be unaccomplished, limited and separate.

A being may "believe" itself to be a... snake, but in reality it has always been and always will be the... rope.

It may enclose and limit itself, if it sees fit, but this will always be in terms of relativity, of appearance; it may consider itself a man, a *Deva*, or anything else, but it remains *Brahman*, that appears to be this or that.

«It is through the power of *māyā* that *Brahman* appears to be the universe» says the *Veda*.

The greatest tragedy which may befall a living being, according to the concepts of some evolutionist doctrines, is that of being *created* by a supreme Entity for the simple purpose of infinite evolving; thus he is forced to elevate himself in order to expand his consciousness more and more in a *horizontal direction* and seek greater perfection, which in any case remains relative because the progression towards perfection is to infinity. An entity, however much it may elevate itself or expand, is faced with a further step to climb; although higher than the preceding one, it will always be lacking and imperfect in comparison to the next one.

In other words, what is asserted is absolute dualism: on the one hand a Perfect being (it has to be admitted if one postulates perfectible beings), on the other, a multiplicity, created by it, imperfect or infinitely perfectible, without end, without hope of complete maturity.

And a being, knowing *a priori*, that its "forced" destiny is unending imperfection, therefore incompleteness and conflict, cannot, law permitting, but stop where it is, in the place or step it is already on, refusing that process of evolution to infinity, since it is a pointless procedure, or worse still, a tragic hoax. Between an imperfect human individual and a Logos-Being, or an even more excellent imperfect Being, it is advisable to stay a human individual, if nothing else for the lesser degree of responsibility involved.

Posing the question of evolution in terms of "more and more", of a "hierarchical or spiritual career", can only give rise to a sense of weariness, of tension and even of competition in the entity's consciousness.

When beings are dragged and forced to grow beyond proportion in a spiral of perpetual, never-ending becoming, obliged to take on more onerous and important tasks and responsibilities, life becomes a struggle, an anguish without even the consolation of a solution.

Other evolutionists maintain, on the contrary, that beings, born imperfect and incomplete, by evolving in time-space, will reach absoluteness. They concede something more than the previous evolutionists, but their Absolute depends on *time*. The term "becoming" here is appropriate because, in truth, the zero-being is not Absolute but "will become" it. In other words, for these evolutionists time, or becoming, leads to Being: but the Buddha, in agreement with all Traditions, maintains that by "going" one never arrives. According to Aristotle a duration without end does not make better what is already good, nor whiter what is already white.

But how can one become if one is not already? And if one is already there is no reason to become. If the term evolution means passing from one state of *nature* to another, this means invalidating the principle of identity of being, which goes against reason because a thing whose nature is A cannot be transformed into another whose nature is B. A minus cannot become a plus, and a non-God a God.

If a being does not contain within itself the potentiality of Being, it will never reach the state of Being. Furthermore, time-space is nothing but a mental "figment", a system of coordinates which responds to a certain category of thought.

The supreme Principle cannot depend on time-space-cause conditions because it does not live on mental categories. The Absolute or Infinite is total fullness, complete in itself. Becoming leads to becoming and Being leads to Being. A quantity of ignorance plus another quantity of ignorance may only become two quantities of ignorance, never knowledge.

In becoming, and by theorizing on becoming, one necessarily postpones the fundamental problems of being. Whoever wishes to emerge from becoming-movement-change (*saṁsāra*) must *stop*, must be reintegrated within the "immobile Mover" which, by its presence alone, gives life to all *appearances*.

The Absolute, as already mentioned, is not infinite time, seen as an unlimited succession or duration, nor is it infinite space, seen as infinite measure (these are always upon the plane of relativity), but the supreme Principle, in its truest sense, is timeless, spaceless, without-a-second. In his *Physics* Aristotle states that the supreme Principle must be *immobile* because only the immobile is absolute cause of the mobile. To explain every movement a principle in itself unmoving must be admitted.

A datum common to the evolutionists, but this is an inevitable consequence, is to consider "experience" as a basic and indispensable factor for evolution, advancement, progress.

Experience, that is a procedure of the empirical and dualistic order, cannot lead to Being, to the Non-Agent, to the immobile Mover.

Being cannot depend on things belonging to the contingent, phenomenal or *māyā* dimension, because it does not depend, as we already said, on time-space-cause.

Empirical experience is the effect of action, it is the fruit of deed; to experience means to move. Action is *karma*, in the broadest sense, and *karma* and *avidyā* are inseparable factors leading to transmigration.

Action-*karma* is restless desire and hunger for possessions which act as support and justification to the perpetuation of the ego.

Action-experience implies extroversion, emergence from one's *aseity*, but the realization and fulfilment are not to be found outside Being; Being is realized only through an act of immediate awareness, of "enstasis" (inwardly abiding) that is not the outcome of action or experimentation, but of "Contemplation", of "Seeing", of "Knowing"; nor, again, is it possible to relate the realization of Being back to a sensorial experience.

Let us say that a being, once it is projected outside of itself, "forgets" its natural state and forces itself into the experience of *saṁsāra* (the myth of Narcissus), but it is when experimenting ceases that being, turning back within itself, discovers itself as motionless Being.

Empirical experience, rather than an instrument of ascesis, is an instrument which perpetuates the Being-becoming duality.

We can state that true experience leads to the recognition of non-experience, to the recognition of the need to die to experience, and this is an aspect of *Śiva*, because *Śiva* is the principle beyond all form, beyond names, beyond experimentation. As a result, liberation-realization does not imply a "motion", a "changing into other", it does not involve a self-altering, a self-mutation, but only a *self-comprehending*, a *self-recognizing*, a *Being*.

100. *Having realized that State (of supreme Reality) which is inscrutable, profound, without birth, uniform, pure and non-dual, we pay our homage to it.*

OM OM OM

MĀṆḌŪKYAKĀRIKĀ

Sanskrit text

Āgama Prakaraṇa

om ity etad akṣaram idaṁ sarvaṁ tasyopavyākhyānaṁ bhūtaṁ bhavad bhaviṣyad iti sarvam oṁkāra eva |
yac cānyat trikālātītaṁ tad apy oṁkāra eva || I ||

sarvaṁ hy etad brahmāyam ātmā brahma so'yam ātmā catuṣpād || II ||

jāgaritasthāno bahiṣprajñaḥ saptāṅga ekonaviṁśatimukhaḥ sthūlabhug vaiśvānaraḥ prathamaḥ pādaḥ || III ||

svapnasthāno 'ntaḥprajñaḥ saptāṅga ekonaviṁśatimukhaḥ praviviktabhuk taijaso dvitīyaḥ pādaḥ || IV ||

yatra supto na kañcana kāmaṁ kāmayate na kañcana svapnam paśyati tat suṣuptam |
suṣuptasthāna ekībhūtaḥ prajñānaghana evānandamayo hi ānandabhuk cetomukhaḥ prājñas tṛtīyaḥ pādaḥ ||V ||

eṣa sarveśara eṣa sarvajña eṣo 'ntaryāmī eṣa yoniḥ sarvasya prabhavāpyayau hi bhūtānām || VI ||

bahiṣprajño vibhur viśvo hy antaḥprajñas tu taijasaḥ |
ghanaprajñas tathā prājña eka eva tridhā smṛtaḥ || 1 ||

dakṣiṇākṣimukhe viśvo manasi antas tu taijasaḥ |
ākāśe ca hṛdi prājñas tridhā dehe vyavasthitaḥ || 2 ||

viśvo hi sthūlabhuṁ nityaṁ taijasaḥ praviviktabhuk |
ānandabhuk tathā prājñas tridhā bhogaṁ nibodhata || 3 ||

sthūlaṁ tarpayate viśvaṁ praviviktaṁ tu taijasam |
ānandaś ca thathā prājñaṁ tridhā tṛptiṁ nibodhata || 4 ||

triṣu dhāmasu yad bhojyaṁ bhoktā yaś ca prakīrttitaḥ |
vedaitad ubhayaṁ yas tu sa bhuñjāno na lipyate || 5 ||

prabhavaḥ sarvabhūtānāṁ satām iti viniścayaḥ |
sarvaṁ janayati prāṇaś ceto 'ṁśūn puruṣaḥ pṛthak || 6 ||

vibhūtiṁ prasavaṁ tv anye manyante sṛṣṭicintakāḥ |
svapnamāyāsvarūpeti sṛṣṭir anyair vikalpitā || 7 ||

icchāmātraṁ prabhoḥ sṛṣṭir iti sṛṣṭau viniścitāḥ |
kālāt prasūtiṁ bhūtānāṁ manyante kālacintakāḥ || 8 ||

bhogārthaṁ sṛṣṭir ity anye krīḍārtham iti cāpare |
devasyaiṣa svabhāvo 'yam āptakāmasya kā spṛhā || 9 ||

nāntaḥprajñaṁ na bahiṣprajñaṁ nobhayataḥprajñaṁ na prajñānaghanaṁ na prajñaṁ naprajñam |
adṛṣṭam avyavahāryam agrāhyam alakṣaṇam acintyam avyapadeśyam ekātmapratyayasāraṁ prapañcopaśamaṁ śāntaṁ śivam advaitaṁ caturthaṁ manyante sa ātmā sa vjñeyaḥ || VII ||

nivṛtteḥ sarvaduḥkhānām īśānaḥ prabhur avyayaḥ |
advaitaḥ sarvabhāvānāṁ devas turyo vibhuḥ smṛtaḥ || 10 ||

kāryakāraṇabaddhau tāv iṣyete viśvataijasau |
prājñaḥ kāraṇabaddhas tu dve tu turye na sidhyataḥ || 11 ||

nātmānaṁ na parāṁś caiva na satyaṁ nāpi cānṛtam ।
prājñaḥ kiñcana saṁvetti turīyaḥ sarvadṛk sadā ॥ 12 ॥

dvaitasyāgrahaṇaṁ tulyam ubhayoḥ prājñaturyayoḥ ।
bījanidrāyutaḥ prājñaḥ sā ca turye na vidyate ॥ 13 ॥

svapnanidrāyutāv ādyau prājñas tv asvapnanidrayā ।
na nidrāṁ naiva ca svapnaṁ turye paśyanti niścitāḥ ॥ 14 ॥

anyathā gṛhṇataḥ svapno nidrā tattvam ajānataḥ ।
viparyāse tayoḥ kṣīṇe turīyaṁ padam aśnute ॥ 15 ॥

anādimāyayā supto yadā jīvaḥ prabudhyate ।
ajam anidram asvapnam advaitaṁ budhyate tadā ॥ 16 ॥

prapañco yadi vidyeta nivarteta na saṁśayaḥ ।
māyāmātram idaṁ dvaitam advaitaṁ paramārthataḥ ॥ 17 ॥

vikalpo vinivarteta kalpito yadi kenacit ।
upadeśād ayaṁ vādo jñāte dvaitaṁ na vidyate ॥ 18 ॥

so 'yam ātmā 'dhyakṣaram oṁkāro 'dhimātraṁ pādā mātrā mātrāś ca pādā akāra ukāro makāra iti ॥ VIII ॥

jāgaritasthāno vaiśvānaro 'kāraḥ prathamā mātrāpter ādimattvād vāpnoti ha vai sarvān kāmān ādiśca bhavati ya evaṁ veda ॥ IX ॥

svapnasthānas taijasa ukāro dvitīyā mātrotkarṣād ubhayatvād votkarṣatīha vai jñānasantatiṁ samānaś ca bhavati nāsyābrahmavit kule bhavati ya evaṁ veda ॥ X ॥

suṣuptasthānaḥ prājño makāras tṛtīyā mātrā miter apīter vā minoti ha vā idaṁ sarvam apītiś ca bhavati ya evaṁ veda ॥ XI ॥

viśvasyātvavivakṣāyāmādisāmānyamutkaṭam ।
mātrāsaṁpratipattau syādāptisāmānyameva ca ॥ 19 ॥

taijasasyotvavijñāna utkarṣo dṛśyate sphuṭam ।
mātrāsaṁpratipattau syādubhayatvaṁ tathāvidham ॥ 20 ॥

makārabhāve prājñasya mānasāmānyamutkatam ।
mātrāsaṁpratipattau tu layasāmānyameva ca ॥ 21 ॥

triṣu dhāmasu yastulyaṁ sāmānyaṁ vetti niścitaṭ ।
sa pūjyaḥ sarvabhūtānām vandyascaiva mahāmuniḥ ॥ 22 ॥

akāro nayate viśvamukāraścapi taijasam ।
makāraśca punaḥ prājñaṁ nāmātre vidyate gatiḥ ॥ 23 ॥

Amātraś caturtho 'vyavahāryaḥ prapañcopaśamaḥ śivo' dvaita evam oṁkāra ātmaiva saṁviśaty ātmanātmānaṁ ya evaṁ veda ॥ XII ॥

oṁkāraṁ pādaśo vidyātpādā mātrā na saṁśayaḥ ।
oṁkāraṁ pādaśo jñātvā na kiṁcidapi cintayet ॥ 24 ॥

yuñjīta praṇave cetaḥ praṇavo brahma nirbhayam ।
praṇave nityayutkasya na bhayaṁ vidyate kvacit ॥ 25 ॥

praṇavo hyaparaṁ brahma praṇavaśca paraḥ smṛtaḥ ।
apūrvo 'nantaro 'bāhyo 'naparah praṇavo 'vyayaḥ ॥ 26 ॥

sarvasya praṇavo hyādirmadhyamantastathaiva ca ।
evaṁ hi praṇavaṁ jñātvā vyaśnute tadanantaram ॥ 27 ॥

praṇavaṁ hīśvaraṁ vidyāt sarvasya hṛdi saṁsthitam ।
sarvavyāpinamoṁkāraṁ matvā dhīro na śocati ॥ 28 ॥

amātro 'nantamātraśca dvaitasyopaśamaḥ śivaḥ ।
oṁkāro vidito yena sa munirnetaro janaḥ ॥ 29 ॥

Vaitathya Prakaraṇa

vaitathyaṁ sarvabhāvānāṁ svapna āhurmanīsinaḥ ।
antaḥsthānāttu bhāvānaṁ saṁvṛtatvena hetunā ॥ 1 ॥

adīrghatvācca kālasya gatvā deśānna paśyati ।
pratibhuddhaśca vai sarvastasmindeśo na vidyate ॥ 2 ॥

abhāvasca rathādīnāṁ śrūyate nyāyapūrvakam ।
vaitathyaṁ tena vai prāptaṁ svapna āhuḥ prakāśitam ॥ 3 ॥

antaḥstānāttu bhedānāṁ tasmāccāgarite smṛtam ।
yathā tatra tathā svapne saṁvṛtatvena bhidyate ॥ 4 ॥

svapnajāgaritasthāne hyekamāhurmanīṣiṇaḥ ।
bhedānāṁ hi samatvena prasiddhenaiva hetunā ॥ 5 ॥

ādāvante ca yannāsti vartamāne 'pi tattathā ।
vitathaiḥ sadṛśaḥ santo 'vitathā iva lakṣitāḥ ॥ 6 ॥

saprayojanatā teṣāṁ svapne vipratipadyate ।
tasmādādyantavattvena mithyaiva svahu te smṛtāḥ ॥ 7 ॥

apūrvaṁ sthānidharmo hi yathā svarganivāsināṁ ।
tānyaṁ prekṣate gatvā yathaiveha suśikṣithaḥ ॥ 8 ॥

svapnavṛttāvapi tvantaścetasā kalpitam tvasat ।
bahiscetogrhītaṁ sad dṛṣtsam vaitathyametayoḥ ॥ 9 ॥

jāgrad vṛttāvapi tvantaścetasā kalpitaṁ tvasat ।
bahiśce togṛhītaṁ sadyuktaṁ vaitathyametayoḥ ॥ 10 ॥

ubhayorapi vaitathyaṁ bhedānām sthānayoṛyadi ।
ka etān budhyate bhedān ko vai teṣāṁ vikalpakaḥ ॥ 11 ॥

kalpayatyātmanā 'tmānamātmā devaḥ svamāyayā ।
sa eva budhyate bhedāniti vedāntaniścayaḥ ॥ 12 ॥

vikarotyaparānbhāvānantaśitte vyavasthitān ।
niyatāniśca bahiścitta evaṁ kalpayate prabhuḥ ॥ 13 ॥

cittakālā hi ye 'ntastu dvayakālāśca ye bahiḥ ।
kalpitā eva te sarve viśeṣo nānyahetukaḥ ॥ 14 ॥

avyakta eva ye 'antas tu sphuṭā eva ca ye bahiḥ ।
kalpitā eva te sarve viśeṣas tv indriyāntare ॥ 15 ॥

jīvaṁ kalpayate pūrvaṁ tato bhāvān pṛthagvidhān ।
bāhyān ādhyātmikāṁś caiva yathāvidyas tathāsmṛtiḥ ॥ 16 ॥

aniścitā yathā rajjur andhakāre vikalpitā ।
sarpadhārādibhir bhāvais tadvad ātmā vikalpitaḥ ॥ 17 ॥

niścitāyāṁ yathā rajjvāṁ vikalpo vinivartate I
rajjur eveti cādvaitaṁ tadvad ātmaviniścayaḥ II 18 II

prāṇādibhir anantais tu bhāvair etair vikalpitaḥ I
māyaiṣā tasya devasya yayāyaṁ mohitaḥ svayam II 19 II

prāṇā iti prāṇavido bhūtānīti ca tadvidaḥ I
guṇā iti guṇavidas tattvānīti ca tadvidaḥ II 20 II

pādā iti pādavido viṣayā iti tadvidaḥ I
lokā iti lokavido devā iti ca tadvidaḥ II 21 II

vedā iti vedavido yajñā iti ca tadvidaḥ I
bhokteti ca bhoktṛvido bhojyam iti ca tadvidaḥ II 22 II

sūkṣma iti sūkṣmavidah sthūla iti ca tadvidaḥ I
mūrta iti mūrtavido 'mūrta iti ca tadvidaḥ II 23 II

kāla iti kālavido diśa iti ca tadvidaḥ I
vādā iti vādavido bhuvanānīti tadvidaḥ II 24 II

mana iti manovido buddhir iti ca tadvidaḥ I
cittam iti cittavido dharmādharmau ca tadvidaḥ II 25 II

pañcaviṁśaka ity eke ṣaḍviṁśa iti cāpare I
ekatriṁśaka ity āhur ananta iti cāpare II 26 II

lokāllokavidaḥ prāhur āśramā iti tadvidaḥ I
strīpuṁnapuṁsakaṁ laiṅgāḥ parāparam athāpare II 27 II

sṛṣṭir iti sṛṣṭivido laya iti ca tadvidaḥ I
sthitir iti sthitividaḥ sarvaṁ ceha tu sarvadā II 28 II

yaṁ bhāvaṁ darśayed yasya taṁ bhāvaṁ sa tu paśyati |
taṁ cāvati sa bhūtvāsau tadgrahaḥ samupaiti tam || 29 ||

etair eṣo 'pṛthagbhāvaiḥ pṛthag eveti lakṣitaḥ |
evaṁ yo veda tattvena kalpayet so 'viśaṅkitaḥ || 30 ||

svapnamāye yathā dṛṣṭe gandharvanagaraṁ yathā |
tathā viśvam idaṁ dṛṣṭaṁ vedānteṣu vicakṣaṇaiḥ || 31 ||

na nirodho na cotpattir na baddho na ca sādhakaḥ |
na mumukṣur na vai mukta ity eṣā paramārthatā || 32 ||

bhāvair asadbhir evāyam advayena ca kalpitaḥ |
bhāvā apy advayenaiva tasmād advayatā śivā || 33 ||

nātmābhāvena nānedaṁ na svenāpi kathañcana |
na pṛthaṅ nāpṛthak kiñcid iti tattvavido viduḥ || 34 ||

vītarāgabhayakrodhair munibhir vedapāragaiḥ |
nirvikalpo hy ayaṁ dṛṣṭaḥ prapañcopaśamo 'dvayaḥ || 35 ||

tasmād evaṁ viditvainam advaite yojayet smṛtim |
advaitaṁ samanuprāpya jaḍaval lokam ācaret || 36 ||

nistutir nirnamaskāro niḥsvadhākāra eva ca |
calācalaniketaś ca yatir yādṛcchiko bhavet || 37 ||

tattvam ādhyātmikaṁ dṛṣṭvā tattvaṁ dṛṣṭvā tu bāhyataḥ |
tattvībhūtas tadārāmas tattvād apracyuto bhavet || 38 ||

Advaita Prakaraṇa

upāsanāśrito dharmo jāte brahmaṇi vartate |
prāg utpatter ajaṁ sarvaṁ tenāsau kṛpaṇaḥ smṛtaḥ || 1 ||

ato vakṣyāmy akārpaṇyam ajāti samatāṁ gatam |
yathā na jāyate kiñcij jāyamānaṁ samantataḥ || 2 ||

ātmā hy ākāśavaj jīvair ghaṭākāśair ivoditaḥ |
ghaṭādivac ca saṅghātair jātāv etan nidarśanam || 3 ||

ghaṭādiṣu pralīneṣu ghaṭākāśādayo yathā |
ākāśe sampralīyante tadvaj jīvā ihātmani || 4 ||

yathaikasmin ghaṭākāśe rajodhūmādibhir yute |
na sarve saṁprayujyante tadvaj jīvāḥ sukhādibhiḥ || 5 ||

rūpakāryasamākhyāś ca bhidyante tatra tatra vai |
ākāśasya na bhedo 'sti tadvaj jīveṣu nirṇayaḥ || 6 ||

nākāśasya ghaṭākāśo vikārāvayavau yathā |
naivātmanaḥ sadā jīvo vikārāvayavau tathā || 7 ||

yathā bhavati bālānaṁ gaganaṁ malinaṁ malaiḥ |
tathā bhavaty abuddhānām ātmāpi malino malaiḥ || 8 ||

maraṇe sambhave caiva gatyāgamanayor api |
sthitaḥ sarvaśarīreṣu ākāśenāvilakṣaṇaḥ || 9 ||

saṅghātāḥ svapnavat sarve ātmamāyāvisarjitāḥ |
ādhikye sarvasāmye vā nopapattir hi vidyate || 10 ||

rasādayo hi ye kośā vyākhyātās taittirīyake ।
teṣām ātmā paro jīvaḥ sayathā samprakāśitaḥ ॥ 11 ॥

dvayor dvayor madhujñāne paraṁ brahma prakāśitam ।
pṛthivyām udare caiva yathākāśaḥ prakāśitaḥ ॥ 12 ॥

jīvātmanor ananyatvam abhedena praśasyate ।
nānātvaṁ nindyate yac ca tad evaṁ hi samañjasam ॥ 13 ॥

jīvātmanoḥ pṛthaktvaṁ yat prāg utpatteḥ prakīrtitam ।
bhaviṣyadvṛttyā gauṇaṁ tan mukhyatvaṁ na hi yujyate ॥ 14 ॥

mṛllohavisphuliṅgādyaiḥ sṛṣṭir yā coditānyathā ।
upāyaḥ so 'vatārāya nāsti bhedaḥ kathañcana ॥ 15 ॥

āśramās trividhā hīnamadyamotkṛṣṭadṛṣṭayaḥ ।
upāsanopadiṣṭeyaṁ tadartham anukampayā ॥ 16 ॥

svasiddhāntavyavasthāsu dvaitino niścitā dṛḍham ।
parasparaṁ virudhyante tair ayaṁ na virudhyate ॥ 17 ॥

advaitaṁ paramārtho hi dvaitaṁ tadbheda ucyate ।
teṣām ubhayathā dvaitaṁ tenāyaṁ na virudhyate ॥ 18 ॥

māyayā bhidyate hy etan nānyathājaṁ kathañcana ।
tattvato bhidyamāne hi martyatām amṛtaṁ vrajet ॥ 19 ॥

ajātasyaiva bhāvasya jātim icchanti vādinaḥ ।
ajāto hy amṛto bhāvo martyatāṁ katham eṣyati ॥ 20 ॥

na bhavaty amṛtaṁ martyaṁ na martyam amṛtaṁ tathā ।
prakṛter anyathābhāvo na kathañcid bhaviṣyati ॥ 21 ॥

svabhāvenāmṛto yasya bhāvo gacchati martyatām |
kṛtakenāmṛtas tasya kathaṁ sthāsyati niścalaḥ || 22 ||

bhūtato 'bhūtato vāpi sṛjyamāne samā śrutiḥ |
niśitaṁ yuktiyuktaṁ ca yat tad bhavati netarat || 23 ||

neha nāneti cāmnāyād indro māyābhir ity api |
ajāyamāno bahudhā māyayā jāyate tu saḥ || 24 ||

sambhūter apavādāc ca sambhavaḥ pratiṣidhyate |
ko nv enaṁ janayed iti kāraṇaṁ pratiṣidhyate || 25 ||

sa eṣa neti netīti vyākhyātāṁ nihnute yataḥ |
sarvam agrāhyabhāvena hetunājaṁ prakāśate || 26 ||

sato hi māyayā janma yujyate na tu tattvataḥ |
tattvato jāyate yasya jātaṁ tasya hi jāyate || 27 ||

asato māyayā janma tattvato naiva yujyate |
bandhyāputro na tattvena māyayā vāpi jāyate || 28 ||

yathā svapne dvayābhāsaṁ spandate māyayā manaḥ |
tathā jāgrad dvayābhāsaṁ spandate māyayā manaḥ || 29 ||

advayaṁ ca dvayābhāsaṁ manaḥ svapne na saṁśayaḥ |
advayaṁ ca dvayābhāsaṁ tathā jāgran na saṁśayaḥ || 30 ||

manodṛśyam idaṁ dvaitaṁ yat kiñcit sacarācaram |
manaso hy amanībhāve dvaitaṁ nopalabhyate || 31 ||

ātmasatyānubodhena na saṅkalpayate yadā |
amanastāṁ tadā yāti grāhyābhāve tadagrahāt || 32 ||

akalpakam ajaṁ jñānaṁ jñeyābhinnaṁ pracakṣate I
brahma jñeyam ajaṁ nityam ajenājaṁ vibudhyate II 33 II

nigṛhītasya manaso nirvikalpasya dhīmataḥ I
pracāraḥ sa tu vijñeyaḥ suṣupte 'nyo na tatsamaḥ II 34 II

līyate hi suṣupte tan nigṛhītaṁ na līyate I
tad eva nirbhayaṁ brahma jñānālokaṁ samantataḥ II 35 II

ajam anidram asvapnam anāmakam arūpakam I
sakṛdvibhātaṁ sarvajñaṁ nopacāraḥ kathañcana II 36 II

sarvābhilāpavigataḥ sarvacintāsamutthitaḥ I
supraśāntaḥ sakṛjjyotiḥ samādhir acalo 'bhayaḥ II 37 II

graho na tatra notsargaś cintā yatra na vidyate I
ātmasaṁsthaṁ tadā jñānam ajāti samatāṁ gataṁ II 38 II

asparśayogo nāmavai durdarśaḥ sarvayogibhiḥ I
yogino bibhyati hy asmād abhaye bhayadarśinaḥ II 39 II

manaso nigrahāyattam abhayaṁ sarvoyoginām I
duhkhakṣayaḥ prabodhaś cāpy akṣayā śāntir eva ca II 40 II

utseka udadher yadvat kuśāgreṇaikabindunā I
manaso nigrahas tadvad bhaved aparikhedataḥ II 41 II

upāyena nigṛhṇīyād vikṣiptaṁ kāmabhogayoḥ I
suprasannaṁ laye caiva yathā kāmo layas tathā II 42 II

duḥkhaṁ sarvam anusmṛtya kāmabhogān nirvartayet I
ajaṁ sarvam anusmṛtya jātaṁ naiva tu paśyati II 43 II

laye sambodhayec cittaṁ vikṣiptaṁ śamayet punaḥ I
sakaṣāyaṁ vijānīyāc chamaprāptaṁ na vicālayet II 44 II

nāsvādayet sukhaṁ tatra niḥsaṅgaḥ prajñayā bhavet I
niścalaṁ niścarac cittam ekīkuryāt prayatnataḥ II 45 II

yadā na līyate cittaṁ na ca vikṣipyate punaḥ I
aniṅganam anābhāsaṁ niṣpannaṁ brahma tat tadā II 46 II

svasthaṁ śāntaṁ sanirvāṇam akathyaṁ sukham uttamam I
ajam ajena jñeyena sarvajñaṁ paricakṣate II 47 II

na kaśij jāyate jīvaḥ sambhavo 'sya na vidyate I
etat tad uttamaṁ satyaṁ yatra kiñcin na jāyate II 48 II

Alātaśānti Prakaraṇa

jñānenākāśakalpena dharmān yo gaganopamān I
jñeyābhinnena sambuddhas taṁ vande dvipadāṁ varam II 1 II

asparśayogo vai nāma sarvasattvasukho hitaḥ I
avivādo 'viruddhaś ca deśitas taṁ namāmy aham II 2 II

bhūtasya jātim icchanti vādinaḥ kecid eva hi I
abhūtasyāpare dhīrā vivadantaḥ parasparam II 3 II

bhūtaṁ na jāyate kiñcid abhūtaṁ naiva jāyate I
vivadanto 'dvayā hy evam ajātiṁ khyāpayanti te II 4 II

khyāpyamānām ajātiṁ tair anumodāmahe vayam I
vivadāmo na taiḥ sārdham avivādaṁ nibodhata II 5 II

ajātasyaiva dharmasya jātim icchanti vādinaḥ
ajāto hy amṛto dharmo martyatāṁ katham eṣyati II 6 II

na bhavaty amṛtaṁ martyaṁ na martyam amṛtaṁ tathā I
prakṛter anyathābhāvo na kathañcid bhaviṣyati II 7 II

svabhāvenāmṛto yasya dharmo gacchati martyatām I
kṛtakenāmṛtas tasya kathaṁ sthāsyati niścalaḥ II 8 II

sāṁsiddhikī svābhāvikī sahajāpy akṛtā ca yā I
prakṛtiḥ seti vijñeyā svabhāvaṁ na jahāti yā II 9 II

jarāmarananirmuktāḥ sarve dharmāḥ svabhāvataḥ I
jarāmaraṇam icchantaś cyavante tanmanīṣayā II 10 II

kāranaṁ yasya vai kāryaṁ kāraṇaṁ tasya jāyate I
jāyamānaṁ katham ajaṁ bhinnaṁ nityaṁ kathaṁ ca tat II 11 II

kāraṇād yad ananyatvam ataḥ kāryam ajaṁ yadi I
jāyamānād dhi vai kāryāt kāraṇaṁ te kathaṁ dhruvam II 12 II

ajād vai jāyate yasya dṛṣṭāntas tasya nāsti vai I
jātāc ca jāyamānasya na-vyavasthā prasajyate II 13 II

hetor ādiḥ phalaṁ yeṣām ādir hetuḥ phalasya ca I
hetoḥ phalasya cānādiḥ kathaṁ tair upavarṇyate II 14 II

hetor ādiḥ phalaṁ yeṣām ādir hetuḥ phalasya ca I
tathā janma bhavet teṣām putrāj janma pitur yathā II 15 II

sambhave hetuphalayor eṣitavyaḥ kramas tvayā |
yugapat sambhave yasmād asambandho viṣāṇavat || 16 ||

phalād utpadyamānaḥ san na te hetuḥ prasidhyati |
aprasiddhaḥ kathaṁ hetuḥ phalam utpādayiṣyati || 17 ||

yadi hetoḥ phalāt siddhiḥ phalasiddhiś ca hetutaḥ |
katarat pūrvam utpannaṁ yasya siddhir apekṣayā || 18 ||

aśaktir aparijñānaṁ kramakopo 'tha vā punaḥ |
evaṁ hi sarvathā buddhair ajātiḥ paridīpitā || 19 ||

bījāṅkurākhyo dṛṣṭāntaḥ sadā sādhyasamo hi naḥ |
na ca sādhyasamo hetuḥ siddhau sādhyasya yujyate || 20 ||

pūrvāparāparijñānam ajāteḥ paridīpakam |
jāyamānād dhi vai dharmāt kathaṁ pūrvaṁ na gṛhyate || 21 ||

svato vā parato vāpi na kiñcid vastu jāyate |
sad asat sadasad vāpi na kiñcid vastu jāyate || 22 ||

hetur na jāyate anādeḥ phalaṁ vāpi svabhāvataḥ |
ādir na vidyate yasya tasya jātir na vidyate || 23 ||

prajñapteḥ sanimittatvam anyathā dvayanāśataḥ |
saṁkleśasyopalabdheś ca paratantrāstitā matā || 24 ||

prajñapteḥ sanimittatvam iṣyate yuktidarśanāt |
nimittasyānimittatvam iṣyate bhūtadarśanāt || 25 ||

cittaṁ na saṁspṛśatyarthaṁ nārthābhāsaṁ tathaiva ca |
abhūto hi yataś cārtho nārthābhāsas tataḥ pṛthak || 26 ||

nimittaṁ na sadā cittaṁ saṁpṛśaty adhvasu triṣu |
animitto viparyāsaḥ kathaṁ tasya bhaviṣyati || 27 ||

tasmān na jāyate cittaṁ cittadṛśyaṁ na jāyate |
tasya paśyanti ye jātiṁ khe vai paśyanti te padam || 28 ||

ajātaṁ jāyate yasmād ajātiḥ prakṛtis tataḥ |
prakṛter anyathābhāvo na kathañcid bhaviṣyati || 29 ||

anāder antavattvaṁ ca saṁsārasya na setsyati |
anantatā cādimato mokṣasya na bhaviṣyati || 30 ||

ādāv ante ca yan nāsti vartamāne 'pi tat tathā |
vitathaiḥ sadṛśāḥ santo 'vitathā iva lakṣitāḥ || 31 ||

saprayojanatā teṣāṁ svapne 'pi vipratipadyate |
tasmād ādyantavattvena mithyaiva khalu te smṛtāḥ || 32 ||

sarve dharmā mṛṣā svapne kāyasyāntar nidarśanāt |
saṁvṛte 'smin pradeśe vai bhūtānāṁ darśanaṁ kutaḥ || 33 ||

na yuktaṁ darśanaṁ gatvā kālasyāniyamād gatau |
pratibuddhaś ca vai sarvas tasmin deśe na vidyate || 34 ||

mitrādyaiḥ saha saṁmantrya prabuddho na prapadyate |
gṛhītaṁ cāpi yat kiñcit pratibuddho na paśyati || 35 ||

svapne cāvastukaḥ kāyaḥ pṛthag anyasya darśanāt |
yathā kāyas tathā sarvaṁ cittadṛśyam avastukam || 36 ||

grahaṇāj jāgaritavat taddhetuḥ svapna iṣyate |
taddhetutvāc ca tasyaiva saj jāgaritam iṣyate || 37 ||

utpādasyāprasiddhatvād ajaṁ sarvam udāhṛtam I
na ca bhūtād abhūtasya saṁbhavo 'sti kathañcana II 38 II

asaj jāgarite dṛṣṭvā svapne paśyati tanmayaḥ I
asat svapne 'pi dṛṣṭvā ca pratibhuddho na paśyati II 39 II

nāsty asaddhetukam asat sad asaddhetukaṁ tathā I
sac ca saddhetukaṁ nāsti saddhetukam asat kutaḥ II 40 II

viparyāsād yathā jāgrad acintyān bhūtavat spṛśet I
tathā svapne viparyāsād dharmāṁs tatraiva paśyati II 41II

upalambhāt samācārād astivastutvavādinām I
jātis tu deśitā bhuddhair ajātes trasatāṁ sadā II 42 II

ajātes trasatāṁ teṣām upalambhād viyanti ye I
jātidoṣā na setsyanti doṣo 'py alpo bhaviṣyati II 43 II

upalambhāt samācārān māyāhastī yathocyate I
upalambhāt samācārād asti vastu tathocyate II 44 II

jātyābhāsaṁ calābhāsaṁ vastvābhāsaṁ tathaiva ca I
ajācalam avastutvaṁ vijñānaṁ śāntam advayam II 45 II

evam na jāyate cittaṁ evaṁ dharmā ajāḥ smṛtāḥ I
evam eva vijānanto na patanti vparyaye II 46 II

ṛjuvakrādikābhāsam alātaspanditaṁ yathā I
grahaṇagrāhakābhāsaṁ vijñānaspanditaṁ tathā II 47 II

aspandamānam ālātam anābhāsam ajaṁ yathā I
aspandamānam vijñānam anābhāsam ajaṁ tathā II 48 II

alāte spandamāne vai nābhāsā anyatobhuvaḥ ।
na tato 'nyatra nispandān nālātaṁ praviśanti te ॥ 49 ॥

na nirgatā alātāt te dravyatvābhavayogataḥ ।
vijñāne 'pi tathaiva syur ābhāsasyāviśeṣataḥ ॥ 50 ॥

vijñāne spandamāne vai nābhāsā anyatobhuvaḥ ।
na tato 'nyatra vijñānān na vijñānān viśanti te ॥ 51 ॥

na nirgatās te vijñānād dravyatvābhāvayogataḥ ।
kāryakāraṇatābhāvād yato 'cintyāḥ sadaiva te ॥ 52 ॥

dravyaṁ dravyasya hetuḥ syād anyad anyasya caiva hi ।
dravyatvam anyabhāvo vā dharmāṇāṁ nopapadyate ॥ 53 ॥

evaṁ na cittajā dharmāś cittaṁ vāpi na dharmajam ।
evaṁ hetuphalājātiṁ praviśanti manīṣiṇaḥ ॥ 54 ॥

yāvad hetuphalāveśas tāvad hetuphalodbhavaḥ ।
kṣīṇe hetuphalāveśe nāsti hetuphalodbhavaḥ ॥ 55 ॥

yāvad dhetuphalāveśaḥ saṁsāras tāvad āyataḥ ।
kśīṇe hetuphalāveśe saṁsāro na prapadyate ॥ 56 ॥

saṁvṛtyā jāyate sarvaṁ śāśvataṁ tena nāsti vai ।
sadbhāvena hy ajaṁ sarvam ucchedas tena nāsti vai ॥ 57 ॥

dharmā ya iti jāyante saṁvṛtyā te na tattvataḥ ।
janma māyopamaṁ teṣāṁ sā ca māyā na vidyate ॥ 58 ॥

yathā māyāmayād bījāj jāyate tanmayo 'ṅkuraḥ ।
nāsau nityo na cocchedī tadvad dharmeṣu yojanā ॥ 59 ॥

nājeṣu sarvadharmeṣu śāśvatāśāśvatābhidhā ।
yatra varṇā na vartante vivekas tatra nocyate ॥ 60 ॥

yathā svapne dvayābhāsaṁ cittaṁ calati māyayā ।
tathā jāgrad dvayābhāsaṁ cittaṁ calati māyayā ॥ 61 ॥

advayaṁ ca dvayābhāsaṁ cittaṁ svapne na saṁśayaḥ ।
advayaṁ ca dvayābhāsaṁ cittaṁ jāgran na saṁśayaḥ ॥ 62 ॥

svapnadṛk pracaran svapne dikṣu vai daśasu sthitān ।
aṇḍajān svedajān vāpi jīvān paśyati yān sadā ॥ 63 ॥

svapnadṛkcittadṛśyās te na vidyante tataḥ pṛthak ।
tathā taddṛśyam evedaṁ svapnadṛkcittam iṣyate ॥ 64 ॥

carañ jāgarite jāgrad dikṣu vai daśasu sthitān ।
aṇḍajān svedajān vāpi jīvān paśyati yān sadā ॥ 65 ॥

jāgraccittekṣaṇīyās te na vidyante tataḥ pṛthak ।
tathā taddṛśyam evedaṁ jāgrataś cittam iṣyate ॥ 66 ॥

ubhe hy anyonyadṛśye te kiṁ tad astīti cocyate ।
lakṣaṇāśūnyam ubhayaṁ tanmatenaiva gṛhyate ॥ 67 ॥

yathā svapnamayo jīvo jāyate mriyate 'pi ca ।
tathā jīvā amī sarve bhavanti na bhavanti ca ॥ 68 ॥

yathā māyāmayo jīvo jāyate mriyate 'pi ca ।
tathā jīvā amī sarve bhavanti na bhavanti ca ॥ 69 ॥

yathā nirmitako jīvo jāyate mriyate 'pi ca ।
tathā jīvā amī sarve bhavanti na bhavanti ca ॥ 70 ॥

na kaścij jāyate jīvaḥ sambhavo 'sya na vidyate I
etat tad uttamaṁ satyaṁ yatra kiñcin na jāyate II 71 II

cittaspanditam evadaṁ grāhyagrāhakavad dvayam I
cittaṁ nirviṣayaṁ nityam asaṅgaṁ tena kīrttitam II 72 II

yo 'sti kalpitasaṁvṛtyā paramārthena nāsty asau I
paratantro 'bhisaṁvṛtyā syān nāsti paramārthataḥ II 73 II

ajaḥ kalpitasaṁvṛtyā paramārthena nāpyajaḥ I
paratantro 'bhiniṣpattyā saṁvṛtyā jāyate tu saḥ II 74 II

abhūtābhiniveśo 'sti dvayaṁ tatra na vidyate I
dvayābhāvaṁ sa buddhvaiva nirnimitto na jāyate II 75 II

yadā na labhate hetūn uttamādhamamadhyamān I
tadā na jāyate cittaṁ hetvabhāve phalaṁ kutaḥ II 76 II

animittasya cittasya yānutpattiḥ samādvayā I
ajātasyaiva sarvasya cittadṛśyaṁ hi tad yataḥ II 77 II

buddhvā 'nimittatāṁ satyaṁ hetuṁ pṛthag anāpnuvat I
vītaśokaṁ tadā 'kāmam abhayaṁ padam aśnute II 78 II

abhūtābhiniveśād dhi sadṛśe tat pravartate I
vastvabhāvaṁ sa buddhvaiva niḥsaṅgaṁ vinivartate II 79 II

nivṛttasyāpravṛttasya niścalā hi tadā sthitiḥ I
viṣayaḥ sa hi buddhānāṁ tat sāmyam ajam advayam II 80 II

ajam anidram asvapnaṁ prabhātaṁ bhavati svayam I
sakṛd vibhāto hy evaiṣa dharmo dhātuḥ svabhāvataḥ II 81 II

sukham āvriyate nityaṁ duḥkhaṁ vivriyate sadā ।
yasya kasya ca dharmasya graheṇa bhagavān asau ॥ 82 ॥

asti nāsty asti nāstīti nāsti nāstīti vā punaḥ ।
calasthirobhayābhāvair āvṛṇoty eva bāliśaḥ ॥ 83 ॥

koṭyaś catasra etās tu grahair yāsāṁ sadāvṛtaḥ ।
bhagavān ābhir aspṛṣṭo yena dṛṣṭaḥ sa sarvadṛk ॥ 84 ॥

prāpya sarvajñatāṁ kṛtsnāṁ brāhmaṇyaṁ padam advayam ।
anāpannādimadhyāntaṁ kim ataḥ param īhate ॥ 85 ॥

viprāṇāṁ vinayo hy eṣa śamaḥ prākṛta ucyate ।
damaḥ prakṛtidāntatvād evaṁ vidvāñ śamaṁ vrajet ॥ 86 ॥

savastu sopalambhaṁ ca dvayaṁ laukikam iṣyate ।
avastu sopalambhaṁ ca śuddhaṁ laukikam iṣyate ॥ 87 ॥

avastv anupalambhaṁ ca lokottaram iti smṛtam ।
jñānaṁ jñeyaṁ ca vijñeyaṁ sadā buddhaiḥ prakīrttitam ॥ 88 ॥

jñāne ca trividhe jñeye krameṇa vidite svayam ।
sarvajñatā hi sarvatra bhavatīha mahādhiyaḥ ॥ 89 ॥

heyajñeyāpyapākyāni vijñeyāny agrayānataḥ ।
teṣām anyatra vijñeyad upalambhas triṣu smṛtaḥ ॥ 90 ॥

prakṛtyākāśavaj jñeyāḥ sarve dharmā anādayaḥ ।
vidyate na hi nānātvaṁ teṣāṁ kvacana kiñcana ॥ 91 ॥

ādibhuddhāḥ prakṛtyaiva sarve dharmāḥ suniścitāḥ ।
yasyaivaṁ bhavati kṣāntiḥ so ’mṛtatvāya kalpate ॥ 92 ॥

ādiśāntā hy anutpannāḥ prakṛtyaiva sunirvṛtāḥ |
sarve dharmāḥ samābhinnā ajaṁ sāmyaṁ viśāradam || 93 ||

vaiśāradyaṁ tu vai nāsti bhede vicaratāṁ sadā |
bhedanimnāḥ pṛthagvādās tasmāt te kṛpaṇāḥ smṛtāḥ || 94 ||

aje sāmye tu ye kecid bhaviṣyanti suniścitāḥ |
te hi loke mahājñānās tac ca loko na gāhate || 95 ||

ajeṣv ajam asaṁkrāntaṁ dharmeṣu jñānam iṣyate |
yato na kramate jñānam asaṅgaṁ tena kīrtitam || 96 ||

aṇumātre 'pi vaidharmye jāyamāne 'vipaścitaḥ |
asaṅgatā sadā nāsti kim utāvaraṇacyutiḥ || 97 ||

alabdhāvaranāḥ sarve dharmāḥ prakṛtinirmalāḥ |
ādau buddhās tathā muktā budhyanta iti nāyakāḥ || 98 ||

kramate na hi buddhasya jñānaṁ dharmeṣu tāyinaḥ |
sarvadharmās tathā jñānaṁ naitad buddhena bhāṣitam || 99 ||

durdarśam atigambhīram ajaṁ sāmyaṁ viśāradam |
buddhvā padam anānātvaṁ namaskurmo yathābalam || 100 ||

GLOSSARY

Abhāva (m): Non-existence. Opposite of *bhāva*.

Adharma (m): Not in conformity with the *dharma*, that which violates the universal Order or the Law (*dharma*).

Adhyāsa (m): Superimposition, substitution. For Śaṅkara: «Appearance in a given place of something which is known from elsewhere, on the basis of imaginative projection».

Adhyātma (n): The supreme Self (*paramātman*), the principial or primordial Self. The intimate Self of all beings.

Adhyātmavidyā (f): The Knowledge of the first principles or of the universal or primordial Self. Supreme Knowledge.

Adhyātmayoga (m): The Supreme *yoga*. The perfect identity with the universal Self.

Adṛṣṭa (a, n): The "not seen", the invisible. Principle non-perceived and non-perceivable by any faculty.

A-dvaita (n): Non-duality, absence of duality. (a): Without-a-second.

Advaita Vedānta: The non-dual *Vedānta*, codified by Gauḍapāda and Śaṅkara. Metaphysical "point of view" (*darśana*) which transcends dualism (*dvaita*) as well as monism (*aikya*).

Advaitin (m): One who follows the *Advaitavāda*, who has realized Non-duality.

Āgama (m): The term means "what has been transmitted", Tradition. In particular it indicates the sacred texts.

Āgamaśāstra (n): Treaties founded on the Scriptures as authoritative interpretation of the *Śruti* (*Vedas* and *Upaniṣads*). It indicates the *Māṇḍūkyakārikā* of Gauḍapāda.

Ahaṁkāra (m): Literally "what makes up the ego", or the "sense of the empirical ego". It constitutes consciousness in the individual state.

Ajāti (f): Non-generation.

Ajātivāda (m): The doctrine of "non-generation" presented by Gauḍapāda in his *kārikās* to the *Māṇḍūkya Upaniṣad*.

Ājñācakra (n): One of the seven *cakras* (lit.: circle), or subtle centers, which express specific states of consciousness. *Ājñācakra* is represented between the eyebrows and has OM as *bījamantra*. It is the center of divine perception or spiritual vision.

Ākāśa (m,n): The "space", the universal ether which pervades the entire universe. It is the first of the five elements (*bhūtas*), its characteristic being *śabda* (sound).

Alātaśānti (f): «The extinction of the burning ember», i.e. the solution of *jīva* into *ātman*. The illusion of the manifold objects, that resolves into the One.

Alātaśāntiprakaraṇa (n): The fourth chapter of Gauḍapāda's *kārikās* to the *Māṇḍūkya Upaniṣad*, entitled: «The extinction of the burning ember».

Amātra (a): Without measure, non measurable in that not subject to experience.

Anāhatacakra (n): One of the seven *cakras*, the one symbolically situated in the heart region. It is the seat of the *jīvātman* in its subtle body.

Ānanda (m): Absolute bliss, pure happiness, joy without objects. Condition that inheres to the awareness of the fulness of one's Being. One of the three inseparable and consubstantial aspects of the Self (*sat, cit, ānanda*).

Ānandamayakośa (m): The sheath of beatitude. The innermost and subjective "casing". The seat of the *jīvā* in the deep sleep state. As it is determined as *kośa* (layer, sheath) it is already in the plane of limitations and therefore does not represent the Brahamanic *ānanda*.

Annamayakośa (m): The sheath of food. The outermost sheath of the Self. Gross sheath. It corresponds to the gross physical vehicle, made up in fact of food, transformed and assimilated.

Antaḥkaraṇa (n): The internal organ, the "mind" in its full extension and various modifications (*vṛttis*) that includes: *buddhi* (intellect, intuitive perception or direct discernment), *ahaṁkāra* (sense of self), *citta* (projecting memory, deposit of subconscious tendencies and predisposition) and *manas* (empirical selective mind).

Apara (a): Inferior, lesser; non supreme, relative.

Aparabrahman (n): Non-supreme or qualified *Brahman* (*Saguṇa*), *Īśvara*. It is the qualified aspect of pure absolute and non-qualified Being (*Nirguṇa*), *Parabrahman* or supreme *Brahman*.

Aparavidyā (f): Non supreme knowledge. Knowledge that concerns the lesser Mysteries or Second Principles.

Aśabda (m): The without sound. Referred to the silent *Brahma*, *Nirguṇabrahma* (without attributes), therefore beyond word-sound.

Asat (n): Non-being; non-reality, what is not nor exists in absolute.

Asparśa (a, n): Without contact, without relation, without support, absolute.

Asparśayoga (m): The *yoga* of "without contact", the pure consciential *yoga* as non mediated realization of the Self.

Asparśin (m): One who has realized the *Asparśayoga*, also one who follows the *Asparśavāda*.

Āśrama (m): Hermitage, life stage. The four life stages in the traditional Hindu society are: *brahmacārya* (celibacy and study), *gṛhasthya* (social and family responsibility), *vānaprasthya* (hermit stage), *saṁnyāsa* (total renunciation). States of consciousness which determine the corresponding life stages.

Ātman (n): Self, Spirit, pure Consciousness, ontological I. *Ātman* is the absolute in us, completely outside of time-space-cause, as such is identical to *Brahman*. Absolute in itself.

AUM (m): The sacred syllable OM (*oṁkāra*) in its constituent elements. It symbolizes the Absolute, see OM.

Avasthātraya (n): The three "states": waking-gross (*Virat*), dream-subtle (*Hiraṇyagarbha*), deep sleep-causal (*Īśvara*) on which the *Vedānta* leads its investigation-discernement (*viveka*) to attain to the ultimate Reality or Fourth (*Turīya*).

Avasthātrayasākṣin (m): Witness of the three states; the Self (*ātman*), pure Consciousness without modifications.

Avidyā (f): Metaphysical ignorance, ignorance with regard to Reality and the noumenon, or the nature of Being. It is the individualized aspect of the universal Ignorance, or *māyā*.

Avyakta (n): The undifferentiated, principial non-manifested condition, universal One, undifferentiated condition of *prakṛti*-substance before it manifests.

Bhakta (m): Devout. One who follows the path of devotion (*bhakti*). Person full of love for the Divine.

Bhakti (f): Ardent devotion, love for the Divine. Participation in the divine Being to the attainment of perfect union with It. For Śaṅkara, *bhakti* is «the constant search for one's real nature». We have *aparabhakti* (non-supreme *bhakti*) and *parabhakti* (supreme *bhakti*).

Bhaktiyoga (m): The *yoga* of devotion. The *sādhanā* rests on filling the emotional body with love so as to cause "breaking through the level", which is necessary to attain the union with the Beloved.

Bhāva (m): Birth, existential world, becoming.

Bhūta (n): The existent, composing or constituting substance; primordial element. First elements of nature. The five sensible elements out of which all bodies are made: earth-solid, water, fire, air, ether.

Bīja (n): Seed, germ, first cause, consciential content.

Bījanidrā (f): Seed-sleep, principial or causal torpor associated with *prājña*. When in it *Īśvara*'s mind (*Māhāt*) projects the universe; awakening from it one can attain *ātman*.

Bindu (n): Point, circle. The symbol of the germinal or principial state, therefore of the undifferentiated unity.

Bindukāraṇa (n): Principial or causal point whence the manifestation geometry emanates, the "seed" of the form.

Brahmā (m): One of the three aspects of the Hindu *Trimūrti* or the threefold form with which the qualified Being, *Brahman Saguṇa* or *Īśvara*, manifests. It is the manifesting principle of the universe that corresponds to the creator aspect, in relation with the conservator (*Viṣṇu*) and the transforming one (*Śiva*).

Brahman or *Brahma* (n): Is the absolute Reality, the *Absolute in itself*. "That" (*Tat*), which is totally transcendent and unconditioned, always identical to itself. One-without-a-second.

Brahman Nirguṇa or *Nirguṇabrahma* (n, m): Non-qualified Reality, free from attributes (*guṇas*), absolute. It is applied to the absolute *Brahman*, see also *Brahman*.

Brahman Saguṇa or *Saguṇabrahma* (n, m): Qualified Being, with attributes (*guṇas*). First qualification of *Brahman* (*Nirguṇa*), see also *Īśvara*.

Brāhmaṇa (n): First of the four traditional social orders (*varṇa*), the priestly one. Liturgical exegesis texts annexed to the *Vedas*.

Bṛhadāraṇyaka Upaniṣad: The "*Upaniṣad* of the great *Āraṇyaka*" one of the oldest and most important vedic *Upaniṣads*. It contains the *mahāvākya* (great word) «*Aham brahmāsmi*: I am *Brahman*».

Buddhi (n): Superior intellect, discerning intelligence, pure reason, intuition of the universal.

Bhūta (n): The existent, composing or constituting substance, elemental, primordial.

Cakra (n): "Wheel", "center". The *cakras* represent determinations of the energy-awareness, or *śakti*.

Caturtha (a): The Fourth. *Caturtha* and *Turīya* have the same meaning and both apply to the Fourth state, the Absolute.

Cit (n): Pure and Absolute Consciousness (*caitanya*), pure Awareness, pure Intelligence, pure Knowledge. *Cit* is beyond any cognitive, representative process, beyond the mental and even beyond pure intellection or intellectual intuition (*buddhi*); yet it gives life to the mind itself, it provides support to its modifications and its functioning. One of the three inseparable and consubstantial aspects of the Self (*sat*, *cit*, *ānanda*).

Darśana (n): Occasion in which to contemplate a Sage. "Point of view", the term is used in relation to the *Veda* doctrine, and to the six orthodox school of Hindu traditional philosophy. The six school are: *Sāṁkhya, Yoga, Vaiśeṣika, Nyāya, Pūrva Mīmānsā* and *Uttara Mīmānsā* or *Vedānta.*

Deva (m): One who is resplendent, angelic being, Deity.

Dharma (m): Stems from the *dhr* root, which indicates supporting, preserving, "wearing", it designates in general terms a "way of being", i.e. the essential nature of a being. Therefore, conformity with the Principle in accordance with the universal law of Harmony-Equilibrium. In metaphysical terms, that through which Harmony manifests as expression of the Unity of Being. In the individual order it relates to the action which one will be able to perform in accordance with the Principle (*karma-dharma*), to attain liberation. Fundamental *dharma* of each human being is to become aware of and to realize in practice one's own divine Nature, which permeates all beings.

Dṛgdṛśyaviveka: «Discernment between the spectator and the spectacle», i.e. between the Self and the non-Self. Title of a fundamental work for in-depth comprehension of the *Advaita Vedānta, a*ttributed by many to Śaṅkara.

Dvaita (n, a): Duality, dualism; dualistic school; dual.

Gauḍapāda: Master of the *Advaita Vedānta* of which he was the first codifier. Śaṅkara's spiritual Master. Author of the *Māṇḍūkyakārikā* (or *Gauḍapādīyakārikā*), verse commentary to the *Māṇḍūkya Upaniṣad*, where the *Ajātivāda* (doctrine of the non-generation, non-creation) and the *Asparśayoga* (*yoga* of no support) are exposed.

Guṇa (m): "Thread", "rope", "constituent quality", (pl. *guṇas*): principial attributes of *prakṛti*-substance or qualitative principles of the universal substance which are at the base of manifestation.

Guru (m): Instructor, spiritual Teacher (*ācārya*), one who removes (*ru* stands for removing) ignorance (*gu* stands for obscurity or ignorance). Instructor in the Vedas, performs purifying ceremonies.

Haṭhayoga (m): *Yoga* of the physiological well-being. It has as its goal perfection and dominion of the body, for its transformation into Temple of the Spirit.

Hiraṇyagarbha (m): Golden germ, cosmic egg (*brahmāṇḍa*). The second of the three states of Being. The totality of the subtle universal manifestation, which comprehends its individual corresponding subtle aspect (*taijasa*).

Indriya (n): Literally "power", indicates both the faculty of the senses and their corporeal organs. Together they constitute an instrument of knowledge (*jñānendriya*) and of action (*karmendriya*). The internal modification of the mind associated with the sensorial organ itself.

Īśvara (m): "Divine Person", it represents what we could define as the personified God. It is the first determination of the absolute *Brahman*, and it comprehends the entire field of manifestation: gross, subtle and causal, both from the cosmic and the individual point of view.

Jāgrat (n): Waking state. The other ones are: *svapna* or dream state, *suṣupti* dreamless sleep state and *Turīya*, which transcends them all.

Jīva (m): Living being (*jīvin*), individuated Soul, consciential reflection of the *ātman* on the universal plane. It produces movement and activity within itself and engenders, through *ahaṁkāra*, the subject (self-*aham*) as well as the object (world-*idam*) of experience, of knowledge.

Jīvanmukta (pp): "Liberated during life", one who has extinguished the threefold Fire.

Jīvātman (m): The *ātman* reflected in the *jīva*.

Jñāna (n): Knowledge, from *jñā* (to know), identical to the greek *gnosis*. Cathartic, liberating knowledge. Also one of the qualities of the Lord (*Bhagavad*): wisdom, intelligence.

Jñānayoga (m): The *yoga* of Knowledge. Its postulates are: intuitive discernment (*viveka)* between real (Self-*ātman)* and non-real (empirical self, non-Self), detachment (*vairāgya*) and reintegration into the Absolute through Knowledge-awareness.

Jñāni (m): Knower, one who practices the *Jñānayoga*, realized being.

Kāma (m): Desire, coveting, greed, attachment to the sensorial world.

Kāma-manas (n): Mental condition of complete conformity with desire; relationship between desire and empirical mind; emotion that proceeds from imagination. It is the characteristic of *manomayakosa*.

Kāraṇa (n): Cause, origin, causal principle.

Kārikā (f): Verse, commentary in verses of a philosophical, ritual, teaching.

Karma or *Karman* (n): Action, activity, principle of causality, effects resulting from an action; rite. It is the inertia of the mental mass of the subject which pushes it to act, think, identify and be in a specific condition. It can be considered as "cause" and as "effect" of the action, which forces the being into perennial becoming (*saṁsāra*).

Kośa (m): Shell, envelope, sheath, energetic sheath. According to *Vedānta* five sheaths envelop the Self: *ānandamayakośa*, *vijñānamayakośa*, *manomayakośa*, *prāṇomayakośa* and *annamayakośa*.

Kuṇḍalinī (f): Literally the "rolled up". Serpentine force; nervous and psychic force placed in the lotus at the base of the spine (*mūlādhāracakra*).

Laya (m): Dissolution-transformation, destruction, absorption (see *Pralaya*).

Liṅga (n): Subtle character, reason. Phallus as symbol of energy. Its elliptic form with its two poles represents the Diad, the bipolarity expressed in creation.

Māhāt (n): The "Great"; cosmic Intelligence; the great Mind. Principle of the cosmic manifestation according to the *Sāṁkhya* darśana. First effect of *mūlaprakṛti*.

Māna (n, m): Opinion, concept; pride, egoism; respect, consideration.

Manas (n): Mind, internal sense, individuated empirical mind endowed of rational-analytical ability, imaginative mind.

Manomayakośa (m): The sheath constituted by the empirical mind, selective-instinctual mind that operates through attraction-repulsion. In it the sense of ego (*ahaṁkāra*) is active.

Mantra (m): Section of the *Vedas*, power words or sounds, hymns used in ritual acts, sacred word, formulae or verses expressed or meditated on during concentration and meditation, vibrating thought.

Manvantara (m): Period of *Manu*, cosmic cycle that comprehends four *yugas*: *satya*, *tretā*, *dvāpara*, *kali*.

Mātrā (f): "Measure"; metric quantity; length of each foot (*pāda*), in the sense of paragraph, division, part.

Maya (a): Particle meaning: "made of".

Māyā (f): Metaphysical ignorance, the word of names and forms as vital phenomenon; all that is modification superimposed (*upādhi*) on the pure Consciousness of the Self; "conform movement", *Īśvara's* "sleep dream".

Mūlādhāracakra (n): One of the seven *cakras*, situated at the base (*adhara*) of the spine where *kuṇḍalinī* is rolled up. Closely related to the individual principle. Its *bījamantra* is *lam*.

Muni (m): Ascetic person practicing silence. One who knows the value of silence (*mauna*). State of consciousness of one who has realized the non-qualified Absolute.

Nirguṇa (a): Free from *guṇas*, non-qualified, absolute, it is applied to *Brahman*.

Nirguṇabrahma (n, m): see *Brahman Nirguṇa*.

Nirvikalpa (a): Free from differentiation, immutable, absolute, transcendent. It refers to Consciousness of *Brahman* non-dual, eternal and unchanging.

Nirvikalpasamādhi (m): *Samādhi* free from differentiations. Consciousness is totally free from differentiations and, therefore, from duality.

Nyāya (n): One of the six *Brahamanic darśanas*, codified by Gautama in the *Nyāyasutra*. *Nyāya* means "logic", "method", "analytical investigation", and can be said to be a pluralistic realism.

OM: The sacred syllable among all. Symbol of the Absolute, of *Brahman* and also of all the concepts the human being has of the Supreme, the Divine. This syllable is part of almost all mantras. The symbol itself is the symbol of Totality and of absolute Unity (non-duality) and is regarded as sacred in all of India. The syllable OM (*oṁkāra*) is seed of meditation as well as its parts A, U, M which express the gross, subtle and causal planes respectively. OM with "sound" represents the qualified Being, *Brahman Saguṇa*, while the "silent" OM represents the non qualified Being or *Brahman Nirguṇa*.

Pāda (m,n): "Foot" in the sense of paragraph, division, part. "Measure", in rhythmical poetry.

Para (a): Other, different; superior, supreme.

Paravidyā (f): Supreme Knowledge, science of the Greater Mysteries, metaphysical Knowledge.

Prājña (m): Causal body of the human *jīva*. In *prājña* multiplicity and duality are reintegrated into unity of undifferentiated consciousness, as synthesis of knowledge. It also represents the *jīva* in the deep sleep state (*suṣupti*).

Prakaraṇa (n): Chapter, section. Specific work or treaties when comprised of four essential sections: *viṣaya*, *adhikāra*, *saṁbandha* and *prayojana*: i.e. subject of treatment, qualification, connection, practical utility.

Prakṛti (f): nature, universal substance, *natura naturans*, the substance by which all sensible and intelligible forms are made. For *Vedānta* it is the equivalent of *māyā*, *pradhāna* or *avyakta*.

Pralaya (m): Dissolution; return into undifferentiated state; dissolution of the world, or manifestation, at the end of a "day" of *Brahmā* (*kalpa*).

Prāṇa (m): Vital breath, cosmic breath, vital energy.

Prāṇamayakośa (m): Sheath of the vital energy. It is constituted by the subtle energies that keep the gross body alive and active.

Praṇava (m): "That which is pronounced". The sacred syllable OM.

Prasthānatraya (n): Threefold Testimony. Threefold Science of the *Vedānta* constituted by the classical *Upaniṣads*, the *Brahmasūtra* and the *Bhagavadgītā*.

Puruṣa (m): Being, man, person, Self, Spirit. For *Sāṁkhya* is the positive principle correlated to *prakṛti* or negative principle-pole. With its pure presence it stimulates *prakṛti*'s activity. In union with *prakṛti* it stimulates the world. So *prakṛti* manifests the dynamism inherent to *puruṣa*'s staticity.

Purva-Mīmāṁsā: "First Investigation", also known as *Karma-Mīmāṁsā* or *Dharma-Mīmāṁsā*, one of the six *darśanas* of Hindu philosophy. According to it pure dogmatic ritualism is the only means to put human beings in contact with Divinity.

Rajas (n): One of the three *guṇas*, which corresponds to activity, energy, desire, fire, passion and responds to expansion, dynamic movement and development.

Śabda (m): The sound, verbal testimony, qualified aspect of *Brahma* in its sound OM, one of the five *tanmātras*.

Sādhanā (f): Name given to any discipline which is ardently followed with perseverance in order to progress in the spiritual life, ascesis, spiritual effort undergone for realization by the disciple.

Saguṇa (a): With attributes, qualified, it refers to *Brahman* endowed of attributes (*guṇas*) or the qualified Being, first superimposition on *Nirguṇabrahma*. Equivalent to *Īśvara*.

Saguṇabrahman (n, m): see *Brahman Saguṇa*.

Śakti (f): Energy, virtual power of *māyā*, energy of manifestation, dynamic energy induced by the presence of the positive immobile pole (*Śiva*), name of the divine mother as divine primordial energy.

Sākṣin (m): Witness, spectator that does not participate and is detached from experiential events and empirical knowledge. It refers to Self as Witness of the three states.

Samādhi (m): Its etymology means transcendent identity, which transcends the apparent formal distinction; state of union (*yoga*) with the personified Divine (*Īśvara*) and of identity (*aikya*) with the impersonal Divine (*Brahman*) attained by the *yogi*.

Saṁbhuti (f): Production, manifesting expression. One who possesses all the powers (*siddhis*). Manifesting aspect of *Brahman*, Universal Soul or Spirit, *Hiraṇyagarbha*: golden Seed.

Saṁcita karma (n): Delayed effect or result of past actions (*karma*) which has accumulated but not reached maturation and actualization in the present state of realization, which can be easily destroyed.

Saṁkalpa (m): Cosmic cycle, universal era. Faculty of self-determination of the empirical mind (*manas*) or resolution, "desire".

Sāṁkhya (n): «Enumeration» of the twenty five categories, principles or *tattvas*. One of the most ancient *Brahmanic darśanas* that envisions a dualistic realism whose poles are represented by an active principle, *Puruṣa* and a receptive one, *Prakṛti*. It was codified by Kapila. Many of its fundamental notions have been adopted by other *darśanas*, particularly the distinction of *puruṣa* and *prakṛti*, and the conception of the three *guṇas*.

Saṁnyāsin (m): Renouncing ascetic. One who, having comprehended, has renounced everything.

Saṁprasāda (m): Constant and imperturbable serenity. *Pax Profunda*.

Saṁsāra (m): Perennial cycle of becoming; transmigrating within becoming as continual passage through different consciential conditions and therefore of existence; indefinite succession of birth-life-rebirth to which liberation (*mokṣa)* puts an end. It corresponds to the uninterrupted chain of cause-effect, for which karma ties the individual to becoming.

Saṁskāra (m): 1. Preparatory purification rites, for consacration, clothing, etc., preparatory rites in general.
2. Causal "seeds" of action engendered by the tendencies that are present in the mental substance (*citta*) and deriving from experiences, actions, thoughts produced in the present existence as well as in the innumerable prior ones.

Śaṅkara: 1. Codifier of the *Advaita Vedānta*, metaphysical *darśana* which transcends the religious dualism and ontological monism itself. He lived between 788 and 820 a.d.. Compiled important commentaries (*bhāṣyas*) to numerous *Upaniṣads*, to the *Bhagavadgītā*, the *Brahmasūtra* and other works in which he summarizes the teaching and the practice through which to attain *Advaita* realization. He was a disciple of Govindapāda who in turn was a disciple of Gauḍapāda. He established himself as a strenuous defender of the *Sanātanadharma*, the Doctrine of the pure vedic Tradition, and instituted ten monastic orders to prevent degeneration of spiritual practice. With the codifying of *Advaita* he provided a solid ontological and metaphysical base for all the cults of the time. He founded four monasteries-*maṭhas* at the four cardinal points of India, focal points of the very powerful influence still perceived today.
2. (m): "He who donates every sort of good", name of *Śiva* that means auspicious, propitious, benevolent, giver of joy and prosperity. *Śiva* is *Śaṅkara*, he who with his Grace causes *saṁ*, or *ānanda* at the highest level.

Śāstra (n): Code, teaching, sacred text. It indicates all sacred Scriptures in general.

Sat (n): Being, pure Being. Absolute and pure existence, contrary to *asat*: that which has no existence. *Sat, cit, ānanda* are the three consubstantial aspects of Being.

Sat-cit-ānanda: Absolute Existence (*sat*), Consciousness (*cit*) and Bliss (*ānanda*). The three consubstantial aspects of *Brahman* and therefore of *ātman*.

Sattva (n): Being, existence in itself, essence, wisdom, "intellectual light", one of the three *guṇas* (the other two are *tamas* and *rajas*) which corresponds to equilibrium, harmony, light, purity. In the hierarchical order of manifestation it corresponds to the causal plane, *tamas* to the gross and *rajas* to the subtle one.

Savikalpa (a): With differentiation, that which contains in itself differentiation, differentiated, formal.

Savikalpa samādhi (m): Transcendental contemplation in which the distinction of subject and object is still latent. It leads to the realization of *Brahman Saguṇa*.

Śiva (m): Beneficial, propitious, one of the three aspects of the *Trimūrti*. The Divine when considered in its transforming and resolving aspect (*mūrti*), but when in union with its *śakti* (*Pārvatī*) takes the function of creator; as such it is symbolized by the *liṅga*. Śivaism separates the aspect of creating from those of conserving and dissolving, so that the aspects that *Śiva* takes and those of the corresponding *śakti* are differentiated, but *Śiva* at the same time is considered as the sole and absolute Principle. For *Vedānta* it is the always and everywhere present One-without-a-second, i.e. *Brahman*.

Smṛti (f): Remembered, indirect or "mediated" Tradition.

Sparśa (m): Contact, relation.

Śruti (f): Audition, the Tradition of the "Heard", sacred Knowledge which was "immediately" revealed (*Veda*), what was heard by the ancient Seers (*Ṛṣis)* as divine Sounds. One of the names given the *Vedas*.

Suṣupti (f): State of deep sleep. Sleep without dream, corresponds to the causal body-plane.

Sūtra (n): Thread, rope; aphorism, verse. Text that codifies the fundamental principles of philosophical *darśanas*. Metaphorically, *ātman* that connects all existential planes.

Sūtrātma (n): Thread of the Self; word that equates to *Hiraṇyagarbha*, subtle universal aspect which comprises the different individualities. Consciential "continuity" of the Self.

Svapna (n): Dream, dream state.

Taijasa (m): "Luminous", from *tejas* (fire), the second quarter, *pāda* (foot) of *ātman*. It constitutes the subtle plane of formal manifest existence and therefore the threefold subtle body (*sūkṣmaśarīra*). It corresponds to *Hiraṇyagarbha* in the universal order.

Tamas (n): One of the three *guṇas* (the other two are *rajas* and *sattva*), which corresponds to obscurity, inertia, passiveness, to inert staticity, etc. It faces "down", it corresponds to ignorance (*avidyā*), representing the maximum condensation of the potentiality of the being. In the hierarchical order of manifestation it corresponds to the gross plane, *rajas* to the subtle and *sattva* to the causal one.

Tapas (n): Heat, ascetic heat, austerity; ardent aspiration, one of the five *niyamas* of *Patañjali*'s *Rājayoga*.

Tattva (n): "Quiddity", truth, principle; category, elemental principle. The twenty five principles, categories in the *Sāṁkhya darśana*, and the twenty six in the *Yoga darśana*.

Turīya (a, n): The Fourth, "Fourth state" (*Caturtha*) which is real absolute and constitutes the necessary non-dual substratum of all relative states and their contents. *Turīya* is *Nirguṇabrahma* and represents the Absolute, Infinite, metaphysical Zero. It can be described only by negations: Non-born, Non-caused, Non-limited, Non-conditioned, Non-determined. It is One-without-a-second (*advaita*) that comprehends and transcends all duality and even principial-ontological unity itself (*Īśvara).*

Upādhi (m): Superimposition, what is superimposed on the Self constituting thereby a "vehicle" and a conditioning at the same time.

Upaniṣads (n): "Sessions or esoteric teachings". Act of "sitting next to someone" in reverential attitude, referring to the disciple at the feet of the Master receiving esoteric knowledge, secret wisdom. For Śaṅkara their purpose is to destroy ignorance-*avidyā*, by providing means apt to attain supreme Knowledge.

Uttara Mīmāṁsā: "Successive Investigation", also known as *Brahma Mīmāṁsā* or *Śarīraka Mīmāṁsā* , it concerns *brahmavidyā*; it constitutes *Vedānta.* One of the six primary Hindu schools. Its doctrine derives from the *Upaniṣads* and was codified by Bādarāyaṇa, traditionally made coincide with Vyāsa, in the *Brahmasūtra* or *Vedāntasūtra.*

Vairāgya (n): Detachment from every form of fruit of action, from all conditions and all objects of attachment; renunciation founded on personal reflection and on the teaching from the *guru.*

Vaiśeṣika: One of the six *darśanas* of the Hindu philosophy, codified by Kanāda. It constitutes the "distinctive doctrine", analysis of the existent. It aims, as the other *darśanas*, to liberate the individual consciousness from the bondage of ignorance.

Vaiśvānara (m): Totality of existence at the gross state of manifestation. Gross totality (*Virāṭ*). It corresponds on the universal plane to the individual gross-physical body (*viśva).* First state of Being described in the *Māṇḍūkya Upaniṣad*: Self in the waking state.

Vaitathya: Apparent, illusory.

Vāsanā (f): Subconscious mental impression induced by experience, action and thought, or arising out of indefinite epochs of the past through accumulated *karma*. "Furrows" in the mental substance (*citta*), they constitute the true "seeds" (*saṁskāras*) of thought, and also of rebirth.

Veda (m): Literally "what has been seen, realized by sages (*Ṛṣis*)"; supreme Knowledge, sacred Science. The four great collections: *Ṛg Veda, Sāma Veda, Yajur Veda* and *Atharva Veda*, contain the exposition of that sacred and traditional Science in its highest expressions and form the *Śruti*.

Vedānta (m): "The accomplishment of the *Vedas*". One of the six *darśana*, also called *Uttara Mīmāṁsā*, it has three currents:
1. *Advaita Vedānta* (non-dualism) codified by Śaṅkarācārya;
2. *Viśiṣṭādvaita*, also *Dvaitādvaita* or *Bhedābheda* (mitigated or modified monism) codified by Rāmānuja;
3. *Dvatavedānta* (dualism) codified by Madhva.

Vidyā (f): Knowledge of Reality; consciential meditation that leads to realization, classified as lower (*apara*) and higher (*para*). The *aparavidyā* is in relation with the first three ends of the human being: *dharma* or rectitude, *artha* or well being, *kāma* or legitimate desire. The *paravidyā*, expounded in the *Upaniṣads*, regards the ultimate end of the human being: *mokṣa* or liberation.

Vijñāna (n): Pure intellect, synonym of *buddhi*, as "synthetic-integrating knowledge" in relation with *manas*. Also Knowledge in the sense of awareness.

Vijñānamayakośa (m): Sheath made of intellect, case of superior intellect, or *buddhi*. Its nature is represented by intellective reason, intuitive discernment. When developed it balances *manomayakośa*, when made "*sattvic*" it is able to contemplate universal archetypes.

Virāṭ or *Virāj* (m): The totality of the gross manifestation (*vaiśvānara*).

Viśva (n): Represents totality of gross manifestation; consciousness waking state in the individual order.

Viveka (m): Intuitive discernment, discrimination between real and non-real, noumenon and phenomenon, which leads to detachment (*vairāgya*) from the non-real and to the becoming conscious of Reality.

Vivekacūḍāmaṇi: "The Great Jewel of discernment", title of a work by Śrī Śaṅkarācārya which is a fundamental text for the realization of the *Advaita Vedānta*. In it a dialogue takes place between a Master and a neophyte where all the principal aspects of the doctrine of Non-duality are thoroughly researched in a highly philosophical and poetical way, in both cognitive and operative aspects.

Yajña (m): Ritual sacrifice. For the Hindu Tradition the entire manifestation is a sacrifice of *Puruṣa* and the human beings must gain inspiration from it in order to reproduce it in the individual order.

Yoga: 1. One of the six *darśanas*, it represents the "doctrine of Union", it is not only a philosophy but proposes operative means to attain "Union".
2. (m): Union, reintegration, complete fusion. Generally the reintegration of the individual into the universal, of the relative (*jīva*) into the absolute (*ātman*).

Yogi or *Yogin* (m): One who practices *yoga*, who is advanced in *yoga*, who has attained Union, i.e. is reintegrated in the Self.

ABOUT RAPHAEL

RAPHAEL is an author and a teacher in the western Metaphysical Tradition as well as in the Vedānta one. Right from childhood he felt a calling towards transcendence. While at College he came across some texts of the Orphic Tradition and of Plato which left a deep impression on him. He then came into contact with the *Vedānta* Tradition. Gauḍapāda and Śaṅkara became his spiritual guides, as though a link that once existed had been restored.

Raphael has spent a substantial number of years writing and publishing on the spiritual experience, commenting and comparing the Orphic Tradition with the work of Plato, Parmenides and Plotinus, for the western Tradition. In the eastern one he is the author of several books on the pathway of non-duality (*Advaita*). He has also translated a number of key vedantic texts from the original Sanskrit, with the addition of his uniquely perceptive commentaries.

He interprets the spiritual practice as a "Path of Fire". Here is what he writes: «... The "Path of Fire" is the pathway each disciple follows in all branches of Tradition; it is the Way of Return. Therefore, it is not a particular teaching of an individual, nor a path parallel to the one and only Main Road... After all every disciple follows his own "Path of Fire", no matter which Branch of Tradition he belongs to».

For Raphael it is important to express through living and being the truth that one has been able to contemplate. The expression of thought and action must be coherent and in agreement with each being's own and specific *dharma*.

In his lifelong activity he has met with many Indian *Swāmis* and *Gurus*, and he has held "conversations" in Germany, France, Italy, Switzerland and in the U.S.A. on Śaṅkara, Plato, Parmenides and Plotinus as well as on aspects of a purely metaphysical order.

After more than thirty-five years of teaching, both oral and in writing, Raphael is now following only those people who wish to be "doers" rather than "sayers", according to St. Paul's expression.

Founder of the Āśram Vidyā Order, he is now dedicating himself entirely to the spiritual practice. He lives in a hermitage connected to the Āśram and devotes himself completely to a vow of silence.

Raphael is connected with the maṭhas founded by Śrī Ādi Śaṅkara at Śṛṅgeri and Kāñcīpuram as well as with the Rāmaṇa Āśram at Tiruvannamalai.

May the Raphael Consciousness, authentic expression of the traditional Metaphysics, guide and illumine along this *Opus* all those who donate their *mens informalis* to the attainment of the highest known Realization.

BOOKS BY RAPHAEL

and related publications

Books by Raphael published in English

The Pathway of Non-duality,
Advaitavāda
Motilal Banarsidass, Delhi 1992

Pathway of Fire,
Initiation to the Kabbalah
S. Weiser, York Beach, Maine, U.S.A. 1993

Essence and purpose of Yoga,
The Initiatory Pathways to the Transcendent
Element Books, Shaftesbury, U.K. 1996

Initiation into the Philosophy of Plato
Shepheard-Walwyn (Publishers) Ltd., London 1999

The Threefold Pathway of Fire
The Aurea Vidyā Foundation, Inc., New York 2000

At the Source of Life
The Aurea Vidyā Foundation, Inc., New York 2001

Beyond the illusion of the ego
The Aurea Vidyā Foundation, Inc., New York 2001

Tat tvam asi, That thou art,
The Path of Fire According to the Asparśavāda
The Aurea Vidyā Foundation, Inc., New York 2002

Māṇḍūkyakārikā *, Gauḍapāda
The Māṇḍūkya Upaniṣad with the verses-kārikās of Gauḍapāda and commentary by Raphael.
The Aurea Vidyā Foundation, Inc., New York 2002

Other Publications
in English

Ātmabodha *, Śaṅkara
Self-knowledge
Edizioni Āśram Vidyā, Roma 1986

Self and Non-Self *
The Drigdriśyaviveka attributed to Śaṅkara
Kegan Paul International, London 1990

Forthcoming Publications
in English

Aparokṣānubhūti *, Śaṅkara
Self-realization

Vivekacūḍāmaṇi *, Śaṅkara
The Crest-jewel of Discernment

Five Upaniṣads *
Īśa, Kaivalya, Sarvasāra, Amṛtabindu, Atharvaśira

The Bhagavadgītā *

The Regal Way to Realization, Yogadarśana *, Patañjali

Beyond Doubt, Raphael

Orphism and Initiatory Tradition, Raphael

The Science of Love, Raphael

* Translated from the Sanskrit and commented by Raphael